STORIES OF THE BYZANTINES

TITLES IN THIS SERIES:

MYTHS AND LEGENDS

STORIES OF THE BYZANTINES

JEAN DEFRASNE

Translated by Patricia Crampton

Illustrated by Philippe Degrave

BURKE LONDON

First published in the English language September 1967
© BURKE PUBLISHING COMPANY LTD. 1967

Translated and adapted from *Récits tirés de l'histoire de Byzance*
© Librairie Fernand Nathan 1966

222 69685 0 LIBRARY ED.
222 69358 4 CLASSROOM ED.

BURKE PUBLISHING COMPANY LIMITED
14 JOHN STREET ★ LONDON, W.C.1

SET IN MONOPHOTO BASKERVILLE
MADE AND PRINTED IN GREAT BRITAIN
BY WILLIAM CLOWES AND SONS, LIMITED
LONDON AND BECCLES

Contents

List of Colour Plates

I

A Day at the Hippodrome

 ONG before the official proclamation, the whole city had heard the news: the Emperor Anastasius had organised some splendid games for the feast of St. Cyril—March 18th.

On the eve of the great day the preparations at the hippodrome proceeded according to the usual ritual. The Master of the Sacred Palace, escorted by high dignitaries, presented to the director of the games a red pennant which was flown from the top of a mast above the main gate. Then, making the sign of the cross three times, he blessed the arena, the imperial tribune and the amphitheatre where more than a hundred thousand people would soon be sitting. Next, he inspected the stables, examined the horses which were to take part in the twenty-four great races and talked for a long time to the leaders of the rival factions.

The factions! In this year 508, they reigned supreme at the hippodrome, and it was the emperor's task to keep a balance between them. At first there had been four, each called by the name of a colour, and each colour was a symbol: blue for water, green for earth, red for the sun and white for air. But little by little the green had absorbed the red, and the blue the white. Although there were still four teams in each race there were now only two factions: the Greens and the Blues; and naturally all the spectators took the side of one or the other.

Moreover, the factions had developed into real political parties, each with an empire-wide organisation. They numbered thousands of supporters; they elected leaders and fought one another incessantly, not only in the circus but even in the streets.

The Master of the Sacred Palace made his tour of the hippodrome, supervising the condition of the track, the strength of the barriers and the proper operation of the starting mechanism by which the four stalls from which the horses started would be opened simultaneously.

The decisive moment had arrived. The lots were about to be drawn. Four little balls, falling one after another from a metal sphere, determined the position of the competitors, but the order was kept strictly secret. The thousands who were gambling on the results would have given a great deal to know which horse had gained the distinct advantage of the inside track!

Before leaving the hippodrome, the imperial dignitaries walked through the galleries, where a number of statues of ancient Greece were preserved, and also some quite modern works, representing the horses and chariot-drivers who had won great victories and whose memory was revered by the crowd.

Now, although it was only midday, the spectators were arriving. They were perfectly willing to spend the night on the tiered seats in order to reserve the best positions. They brought cushions with them for comfort, umbrellas to protect them from the sun, and baskets of pastries and fruit.

"Who'll buy my lemons, my fine juicy oranges?"

"New honey, fine honey, honey from Lembos . . ."

The vendors passed along the tiers as the spectators argued the favourites' chances:

"Euthymos cannot lose," said one.

"No, no. Icarios is the best," replied another.

"Personally," said a third, "I am putting all my money on Agathon. He has the best beasts of the lot, and the others will be left ten lengths behind!"

The enthusiasts had discussions with those who collected the wagers. They also watched the competitors as they came on to the track to make their last practice runs under the vigilant eye of the trainers, who called out advice:

"Turn shorter, slacken the right rein!"

There was hectic activity among the grooms, the saddlers and the wheelwrights. The sweat-streaked horses were rubbed down, the chariot axles tightened and greased, the reins and bridles adjusted.

The sun went down on a motley and clamorous crowd, united in their love of the games: Byzantines in their long embroidered robes, Syrians in flowing, loose-sleeved gowns, black-robed Jews, desert Arabs dressed in the white burnous, Bulgarians with shaven heads, wearing cloaks of leather or fur, western Franks with their long moustaches, Hungarians from the Steppes, Khazars, Varangians, peasants from the Nile and mountain people from the Caucasus. There were people speaking every language, representing every human type, yet all rubbed shoulders amicably.

As night fell, the sentinels took their turn at guard duty, torch in hand, near the stables where the shouts of men and the whinnying of horses were dying down. Their dark forms blending with the marble steps, the huge crowd fell asleep at last, in confident anticipation of the day of the great game: the moment of delight.

*   *   *

Dawn broke. The town seemed dead. In the shops, workrooms and yards there was not a soul to be seen. The port, too, was deserted. Near the hippodrome the processions were forming, each faction headed by its leaders and banners. There were the young dandies with their bizarre fashions; they wore their hair shaved in front like the Huns, but falling in long ringlets on their shoulders like the Persians; each had a pointed beard, and wore a bright tunic with puffed sleeves, breeches laced about his legs with leather thongs, and a great, flowing cape held by a golden brooch. They carried long shafts tipped with a crescent of cutting metal like a spearhead, and each wore a short sword, the blade naked and shining, at his hip.

Suddenly, shouts and cheers rang through the hippodrome. The factions came through the gate of honour and took the places reserved for them in the amphitheatre—the Blues to the right and the Greens to the left of the imperial tribune. The heads of the two camps made the sign of the cross, while their supporters cheered them, singing at the tops of their voices:

"Hail, lord! May this be your finest day. Hail, the fortunate elect, our well-beloved leader!"

Then the emperor's guards entered the arena in their turn to the sound of music and took their places on a terrace separated from the track by a ditch. Above them was the box of the *Basileus*—the emperor—which was linked directly with the palace by a secret passage. The sun gleamed on the silver breast-plates, the sabres and the tall, embossed shields, while resplendent banners fluttered in the wind.

For the last time the officials inspected the barriers and the barred gates which separated the public from the arena. The crowd grew impatient. Where was the emperor?

Anastasius was well aware that his people awaited him. But in accordance with court ceremonial he carried out the traditional rituals without haste. In his private chapel he lighted candles before the holy icons. Then he received the Master of the Palace, who brought him the most recent reports from the hippodrome, and ended his statement:

"Sire, all is in readiness!"

Then Anastasius walked to a hall decorated with golden mosaic, where he put on a purple mantle and the imperial crown. He took his place at the end of a long gallery and the guards gave passage to the high dignitaries in their appointed order, while the steward chanted the illustrious titles in a loud voice: "Grand Logothete, Protostator, Sacellarius, Eparch . . ."

Then the emperor received the commanders-in-chief, or *strategi*, the town *archons*, or magistrates, and the foreign ambassadors. All prostrated themselves before him, repeating three times:

"Long life to you, Roman Caesar, victorious sovereign . . ."

Turning, Anastasius walked slowly to the imperial box. The servants threw open the bronze double doors; a bell resounded through the hippodrome and the crowd fell silent; the soldiers presented arms; the standard-bearers of the factions waved their green or blue flags. It was a moment of intense emotion.

Then the emperor appeared. Making the sign of the cross three times, he blessed the dense crowd sitting along the tiers. He heard the sound of shouts, singing and cheers rising up to him. Waiting for the noise to die down, he raised his hand in a ritual signal and the games began.

*　　*　　*

There, quite close, was the course—divided in two by a low wall, which measured about two furlongs, and was surmounted by splendid monuments: the obelisk of Theodosius in pink Egyptian granite, a bronze pyramid tipped with silver gilt, a white marble column dedicated to Apollo by the Greek leader Pausanias and bearing the names of the towns which had broken the Persian invasion: Sparta, Athens, Megara.

But, above all, at either end of this central line were the stone markers round which the competitors had to wheel twenty times, turning perilously, as short as they possibly could, before entering the final straight.

They're off! The four gates opened and the light, fast, four-horse chariots were already flinging up the dust. Their drivers stood firmly erect, whip clenched in the teeth, reins in hand, trying to establish a lead in order to round the first marker on the inside. The Blue seemed to be ahead. From the first his horses had galloped easily, with effortless rhythm.

The crowd was exuberant. As lap after lap was raced the Blue gained still more advantage, and his racing partner, the White, was behind him.

"He's winning! He's won!"

The chariots lined up before the imperial tribune. Euthymos, champion of the Blues, waved to his friends, passed down the ranks of the soldiers and reached the emperor, who congratulated him and placed a laurel wreath on his head.

The races continued. By midday the two camps had won an equal number of victories. There was one test left, which promised to be thrilling. The director of the games went over to the excited competitors and talked to them at length, imposing on them the strictest discipline.

The starting signal was given. The spectators rose to their feet. The Green and the Blue were neck and neck.

The two teams were giving their best. The last boundary stone was in sight.

"Agathon! Agathon!"

The Blues chanted the name of their favourite. But suddenly their joy was turned to horror. Agathon, hard-pressed by his adversary, turned too short. The left wheel of his chariot, travelling at full speed, struck the marker and smashed. The Red, close behind, could not turn aside in time; the horses fell and the overturned chariots were shattered. The two men, attached by the reins to their broken teams, were dragged in the blood-stained dust.

Meanwhile, the Green had passed, and now he won easily. A wretched victory, thought the Blues, yelling with fury and cursing the winner, whom they held responsible for the accident. But Anastasius, who had not troubled to conceal his sympathy for the Greens, signified approval. The audience broke into tumult, insults were exchanged, fights started and were quickly suppressed by the guards. Gradually calm was restored. The emperor had withdrawn. The races would not begin again until evening.

Now it was time for the interval. While the amphitheatre staff cleared the course and restored it to order, dancers, jugglers and mimes entered the arena. Dwarfs indulged in extraordinary contortions, wrestlers struggled together, conjurers released pigeons. One acrobat, amid great applause, reached the tip of the great obelisk and balanced there, poised erect on the gilded cone.

Now the animal trainers were filing past: turbaned

Hindus with serpents about their necks, Nubians dark as ebony leading Sudanese lions on chains, Khazars with camels and Bulgarians with wolves.

But the hippodrome bears were not there. Everyone regretted the absence of those beautiful and powerful beasts which, despite their clumsy appearance, could dance gracefully to the sound of the flute. Why were they not there today?

"Have you not heard? Akakius, the bear-leader, is dead."

And there was his widow, in deep mourning. She had let down her long hair and was clawing at her face in grief as she made her way through the crowd, leading her three daughters who held out suppliant hands to the bystanders.

Asterius, the Green leader, spoke brusquely to her:

"Why waste your time? We need a strong man to lead the bears and we have already taken on Akakius' replacement. Get along with you! We are sick of your cries and tears!"

Yet the spectators admired the touching beauty of the three daughters. The eldest, Comito, seemed so distressed that she aroused their compassion. The little one, Anastasia, barely six years old, stretched out her thin, childish arms and tried not to cry. But it was the second who attracted the most attention. Little by little, her name reached the tiers of seats:

"That's Theodora. How lovely she is!"

She was indeed very beautiful, with her delicate face, her great black melancholy eyes and her slender figure. Despite her poor tunic and bare feet, her pale

2

and unkempt appearance, she had the air of a queen, dignified and proud.

"Drive them out of here!" cried Asterius angrily.

So the Greens, following their leader, insulted the widow and her children, while the Blues, always ready to run counter to their enemies, applauded wildly and shouted encouragement.

Theodora walked the length of the course, indifferent to praise and insult alike, holding her sisters by the hand, and reviving her mother's strength and confidence with a look.

But rage swelled in her heart against those who insulted her and whose screams of hatred she could hear. Later, when by a chance turn of fate the bear-leader's daughter became Empress of Byzantium, she was to loathe the Greens and take every opportunity to revenge herself, for she would not forget the contempt they had poured upon her that day at the hippodrome.

2

The Nika Rebellion

ONG lines of carts had been pouring into the market from dawn onwards, delivering grain, vegetables, fruit and jars of wine and oil to the capital. Butchers were slaughtering lambs; fishermen were bringing in huge baskets of fish from the Bosphorus: red mullet, tunny and silver-scaled sturgeon.

Under the arcades, shop doors were opening and craftsmen were setting to work under the interested eyes of the crowd. Every trade was represented; there were weavers, cobblers, potters and smiths. Merchants extolled the quality of their silks; Syrian pedlars offered their perfumes and spices; the men of the desert caravans unrolled deep-pile carpets in vivid colours. As the morning was grey and chill, fires had been lighted in the streets and beggars squatted round them, wailing strange laments.

But what was this sudden commotion? A whisper ran through the town, causing immediate panic:

"There is fighting in the Forum of Constantine!"

Yet another quarrel had broken out between the armed supporters of the two factions. The date was January 11th in the year 532. This time the Greens had the upper hand. They had succeeded in taking a group of the Blues by surprise in the corner of a portico. Insults were exchanged and led to blows, and now a desperate struggle was in progress. The imperial guards, hurriedly warned, ran to the scene while the terrified passers-by fled. The guards immediately fell upon the Greens, broke up their ranks and herded them towards the great avenue, called the Mesé.

The Blues re-formed, in response to their leaders' command, and started to chase the Greens down the narrow lanes of the old town. The guards let them go and returned calmly to the palace. The Blues soon had the advantage and were giving their enemies rough handling.

Near the Square of Taurus there was a fierce scuffle: a booth was ransacked and set alight; a respected merchant, old Alexis, was killed. Who had done it? A Blue? A Green? Each camp accused the other of this crime, which had aroused the indignation of the people. Was the capital of the empire no longer a safe place for honest merchants who took no part in the quarrels of the factions?

In the Sacred Palace the Emperor Justinian was disturbed. He gathered his chief advisers about him.

"The law must be the same for everyone," said

Tribonian the Quaestor. "Neither of the two camps must be able to boast that it enjoys the imperial favour."

"It would be proper for you, sire," added the Prefect of the Praetorium, John of Cappadocia, "to punish those responsible for the disorder, whether they be Greens or Blues."

But Theodora intervened. She loathed the Greens who, for their part, never concealed their contempt for "the bear-leader's daughter".

"The Greens are your enemies, Justinian," she said. "They look back with regret to the days of the Emperor Anastasius who gave in to all their whims, and they are plotting to put one of his nephews, either Hypatius or Pompeius, on the throne. Are we going to let them do it?"

Eudemon, the Town Prefect, and Calopodios, the Captain of the Guard, supported the empress. The Greens were on the point of revolt; precautions must be taken.

After some thought, Justinian made up his mind to go to the hippodrome, where a huge crowd had gathered for the chariot races. He took his seat in the imperial tribune, surrounded by the high dignitaries of the Court. Meanwhile, the Empress Theodora, followed by her ladies-in-waiting, had gone to the church of St. Stephen, where she could watch the entertainment from a gallery with heavily barred windows overlooking the amphi-theatre.

The emperor's arrival was greeted with murmurs. Some cheers were heard, however, and the chief of the Greens spoke in a moderate tone:

"Long life to you, Justinian!"

But complaints quickly followed the greeting:

"We are unjustly treated, do you know that? We are persecuted in the town . . . Our oppressor is there, close to you, but I fear to name him, for he is powerful. May he be accursed for the evil he does to us!"

As the shouts grew louder Justinian called to his side an official in a white toga, who was carrying a silver rod. This was the herald, who would address the people in the emperor's name:

"Why this uproar?" the herald asked the Green leader. "Who has wronged you? Speak without fear!"

The Greens conferred and finally accused Calopodios, the Captain of the Guard, whom they called a Judas. The herald was angered by their boldness.

"So," he said, "you have come here only to insult those who govern you!"

"The man who commits the injustice will suffer the fate of Judas."

"Silence!" cried the furious herald. "Silence, unbelievers, or I will cut off your heads!"

"You have only to listen to us, we speak nothing but the truth."

"Are you not free men?"

"No! We are maltreated and beaten. As soon as anyone in this town is suspected of being a Green he is certain to be punished."

The herald protested and accused the Greens of rebellion. Justinian had risen from his throne and he now faced the screaming crowd. Theodora beat her fists against the bars. She wanted the emperor to set the guards on this insolent faction. Belisarius and Mundus, the two generals who were standing in the official tribune, could not understand why Justinian was allowing one of his closest advisers to be insulted in this way.

Gradually the feeling mounted, insults were exchanged and fists were shaken towards the emperor. But he remained aloof.

"Just let our distinguishing colour be removed," the Green leader retorted, "and the judges can sit back! This morning, Alexis the merchant was killed, but his murderer will go unpunished, for he was not one of us." This was, of course, an implied criticism of the praetorian prefect, who was responsible for the government of the city.

The Blues had kept silent until then, for they were not displeased to hear John of Cappadocia being attacked by the Greens, the faction he was known to support. But now that they were being drawn into the argument, they replied:

"You Greens have murderers all over the stadium!"

"You Blues kill and run!"

"Do you need proof of your crimes? Who slew the merchant?"

"It was you who killed him!"

Now the two factions were confronting each other, flinging the names of their murdered friends at each other's heads, calling for justice and vengeance. The herald grew impatient:

"Blasphemers, enemies of God, when will you be silent?"

The guards lined up before the imperial tribune.

What would the Greens do? Their leader asked for silence and addressed Justinian:

"Since you command it, sire, we will be silent, but against our will. We know all, but we shall not speak. Farewell justice, you reign no longer here below! Farewell to you all, we shall depart. We shall become Jews or pagans, no matter what, but we will never be Blues, as God is our witness."

And the Greens left the hippodrome. The scandal was tremendous. It was the first time that a faction had dared to offer such a slight to the emperor. Theodora was furious. Despite the cheers of the Blues, Justinian could not conceal his anxiety as he returned to the Sacred Palace.

*   *   *

The Greens went up and down the streets, crying:

"Down with Tribonian the Quaestor! Down with the Prefect of the Praetorium, the accursed Cappadocian who burdens us with taxes! Death to Calopodios! Justice for the oppressed people!"

Eudemon the Town Prefect had promised Justinian that he would re-establish order as quickly as possible. Placing himself at the head of the heavily armed guards, he dispersed the crowds and had a number of men arrested at random. Three of them were led before him, trembling with fear.

"Let them be hanged at once!" he ordered, not caring in the least to which faction they belonged.

When this harsh sentence was announced, the people, whom the guards had difficulty in restraining, massed in the Augusteum where the gallows had been erected. The hangman prepared to fulfil his office. The nooses tightened once . . . twice . . . but the next moment the ropes had broken; the first two victims fell to the ground unharmed.

"Have pity on them!" came shouts from every side.

But Eudemon was relentless. He threatened to punish the hangman, and the execution started again. But, as the crowd watched in stupefaction, the two ropes broke again.

"Mercy, mercy! It is God's will!"

The crowd surged forward, overthrowing the guards. They freed the two men and led them to a place of refuge—the church of St. Lawrence. Then they realised that by a stroke of fate one was a Green and the other a Blue; and this reconciled the two camps.

The whole town was now seething with anger. The leaders of the two factions, forgetting their quarrels, conferred together. They demanded an audience of the Prefect of the Praetorium, John of Cappadocia. But the prefect had no wish to lose the imperial favour. He refused. He even dared, in defiance of the law of sanctuary, to have the two condemned men arrested in the church and thrown into prison.

Next day the crowd gathered again at the hippodrome. The chariot races were being continued, in the vain hope of calming tempers. The Greens and Blues at once demanded mercy of the emperor. But Justinian had promised Theodora not to yield. He remained impervious to threats and prayers alike. The onlookers murmured, and the Master of the Palace called on them to pronounce the habitual greeting: "Long life to the all-powerful emperor." Then a violent uproar broke out:

"Long life to the Greens and Blues, united in a plea for mercy!"

As the games ended, rioting spread throughout the town and again and again rose the cry, "*Nika!*"—Victory! The people rushed headlong to the prison and, after releasing the prisoners, they set fire to the building. Then they besieged the walls of the Sacred Palace, demanding the dismissal of the emperor's chief advisers.

Justinian was shocked at the violence of the revolt. He withdrew into his private chapel to pray and entreat the help of the Holy Trinity. The opinions of his followers were divided; some counselled force; others advised immediate concessions. "What," asked the latter, "can be done when the storm is raging?"

During the next few days the rebellion engulfed the whole city. The rebels thronged at the gates of the Sacred Palace, yelling their fury.

Justinian was worried. He hesitated to appeal to the garrison which was quartered at the end of the Golden Horn, because he did not trust its commanders. But, by chance, Belisarius (who had just defeated the Persians) and Mundus (who had been fighting the Ostrogoths on the Danube) were in the palace with their personal guards, all champions: the famous *bucellarians*.

"Order must be restored, cost what it may," said Theodora.

So the emperor ordered Belisarius and his troops out against the rebels. But in the battle the priests of St.

Sophia, who were trying to separate the combatants, were struck by the soldiers. The holy relics they were carrying in procession were trampled underfoot.

Sacrilege! The crowd was enraged. From rooftops, windows and terraces, men and women flung down stones and tiles on the soldiers. Belisarius had to order his troops to retreat to the Sacred Palace.

"Victory! Victory!"

The people were in control of the streets. They set fire to the official buildings—the senate, the quaestorium, the library. The fire reached the public baths, the great avenue of the Mesé, St. Sophia and even the vestibule of the palace—the Chalcé.

"Fire! Run!"

The crowd fell back, for the flames were spreading, ravaging the church of St. Irene, the hospital and the forum and attacking luxurious villas and squalid hovels with equal fury.

Rich and poor, united by fear, rushed to the port seeking boats to take them across to the Asian shore. They fought on the banks to find places in vessels whose crews were in a hurry to weigh anchor.

The city lay under a dense cloud of ash and smoke. Fugitives wandered in every direction along the cluttered streets; looters made haste to sack those houses that were still intact. Syrian and Egyptian monks, persecuted by the authorities for their lack of discipline, saw in this fire the vengeance of heaven:

"God be praised!" they said. "Justinian the tyrant is punished."

*　*　*

In the palace one alarming report followed another. The wind had risen; the fire, which had been dying down, sprang up again near the Forum of Constantine. Armed bands roamed the streets and gathered round the hippodrome. The governors of the neighbouring provinces had promised to send reinforcements, but it was impossible for them to arrive in less than ten days, even if all went well.

No, resistance under these conditions was madness. Justinian thought the people loved him. They demanded the dismissal of his ministers and he agreed.

The emperor told the herald to announce throughout the town that Calopodios, the Captain of the Guard, Eudemon, Prefect of the Town, and Tribonian, the Palace Quaestor, had been disgraced. Moreover, the Prefect of the Praetorium, John of Cappadocia, who was so heartily loathed, was to yield his post to a good man, the nobleman Phocas. What more did they want? Had not the people's wishes been fulfilled?

But these concessions came too late. The crowd, not unjustly, interpreted them as signs of weakness.

"Justinian has betrayed the people. He must abdicate."

"We want one of Anastasius' nephews as our leader."

"Blessed be the name of Anastasius! He was a guide to us, a father . . ."

Anastasius' nephews, Hypatius and Pompeius, were far from pleased by these exhortations. As members of the senate, loaded with honours, they had hastened to the palace to assure Justinian of their loyalty. They had even demanded sanctuary, fearing the fury of their supporters.

But the emperor refused. He defied everything and everyone. He wished to be alone. He ordered Anastasius' nephews and the other senators to return to their homes.

"Be calm, as I am," said he, "and the people will see their mistake."

Justinian really thought that the revolt would die down as quickly as it had arisen. He decided that what was needed was a gesture from him. He decided to go to the hippodrome, using a secret corridor from the palace.

The crowd sat there, in the amphitheatre, like the people of a conquered country. Some, driven away by the fire, had taken refuge in the circus with their domestic animals and the few possessions they had been able to save; they seemed exhausted. The others, brandishing arms they had stolen, were planning a decisive assault on the palace.

Suddenly bells rang out. Justinian appeared in the imperial tribune, clad in the imperial purple, carrying a copy of the Gospels in one hand and a silver cross in the other. The crowd looked up in silent amazement.

"I will forgive you," said the emperor, "if you remain calm. I alone am the cause of all this. My sins made me refuse to deal justly with your rightful demands."

The Blues responded to these words with a few timid acclamations:

"Long live the Emperor Justinian!"

But the Greens exploded. They shouted insults:

"Liar! Fool! Perjurer!"

Stones were thrown at the imperial box while they

shouted the name of Hypatius, nephew of Anastasius, the ruler for whom they longed. Justinian, followed by his guards, returned hastily to the palace, trembling with fear and rage.

*   *   *

"Hypatius! We want Hypatius!"

The rebels were thronging to the house of the man they already regarded as their emperor. They dragged him to the forum, despite the tears of his wife Mary who tried to hold him back, groaning:

"No! I beg you, do not accept! They are leading you to your death."

Hypatius tried to resist, but he was powerless against the surging sea of people. Driven by the crowd yelling his name, the unfortunate man found himself in the forum, robed in an imperial mantle stolen from a summer residence of the Basileus. For want of a crown the Greens had placed a golden collar on his head.

Hypatius was led to the hippodrome and installed in the imperial tribune. The banners of the factions, united in rebellion, were raised to the top of the golden quadriga—the four-horse chariot—which Constantine the Great had presented to the people long ago.

"Long life to you, Hypatius, prince of the Romans!"

"Victory! Victory!"

Hypatius, dazed by their cries, swamped by a human sea, did not lose his self-possession. He sent one of his officers, young Ephraim, to the palace:

"Assure Justinian of my loyalty. Tell him that the rebels who forced me to come to the hippodrome are gathered here about me. Tell the emperor to hurry! It will be easy for him to disperse these circus brawlers with a few well-trained troops."

Ephraim hurried to the palace; but he found the gates closed. He tried, in vain, to explain to the guard that he was the bearer of an important message. He was growing desperate. Then he saw a friend coming; it was Thomas, the Court physician, who told him to return to the hippodrome:

"Go and tell Hypatius that the matter is settled here: Justinian has gone."

In fact, he was anticipating events, but it was as good as done. Justinian had told Thomas and his courtiers that he wished to leave the town. For three days the Prefect of the Praetorium, John of Cappadocia, had been secretly preparing ships in the port of Bucoleon to transport them to the Asian shore. He had made careful preparations for the departure of Justinian and Theodora, the palace staff and loyal troops. The treasures of the Crown would, of course, be taken with them.

A last meeting was held at the palace late in the afternoon. Justinian, nervous and excited, thought only of flight:

"Is everything ready? Well, let us make haste to leave this city which God has abandoned to the fury of the wicked. Come, time is pressing!"

The imperial dignitaries, fearing for their lives, rejoiced in the sovereign's decision. They were leaving . . .

No, they were not leaving. The Empress Theodora appeared, very dignified and very calm. She was pale and her eyes burned brightly. Coming forward and observing the general dismay, she spoke in a deliberately grave and measured tone:

"No one should be surprised to see a woman offer counsel at such a time. Since all seems lost, I cannot hold my peace. I am opposed to flight, even if it would save our lives."

Justinian looked embarrassed, but said nothing. All those present bowed their heads as if they had been caught misbehaving. The only exception was the Prefect of the Praetorium, John of Cappadocia. Sensing the danger of this intervention, he shrugged his shoulders and looked unabashed while Theodora continued:

"Those who have worn the crown cannot survive its loss. I could not bear to see the light of day if I were despoiled of the imperial glory. If you wish to flee, Caesar, very well: you have money, the ships are ready, the sea is clear. I intend to stay! And I shall honour the ancient maxim which says: 'The purple makes a noble shroud.'"

Justinian was moved by these vigorous words; soon there was no more talk of departure. One of the empress's followers, the cunning Narses, undertook to separate the Blues from the Greens for gold, if he were given the means. Belisarius and Mundus called up their powerfully armed élite guard. Belisarius even tried to make his way along the secret corridor to arrest Hypatius in the imperial tribune. But the guards no longer knew whom to obey and would not let him pass.

So Belisarius adopted another plan. At the head of two hundred Goths, leading their terrified horses through the flames by the bridle, the young general passed the

The rebels thronged at the gates of the Sacred Palace

church of St. Stephen, the burning quaestorium, the ruined colonnade. He overthrew the militia of the factions and forced an entry into the hippodrome by the Castor and Pollux Gate. Erect upon his white horse, in silver armour and crested helm, a sword gleaming in his hand, he advanced. Confronting the imperial box, he addressed Hypatius:

" Go, accursed usurper! Go, and implore your master's pardon!"

"Glory to Justinian, the elect of God!" chorused the guards.

The Greens were furious. They rushed upon the mounted soldiers, who closed their ranks and repulsed the crowd with some difficulty, using their long spears. The Blues, already partly won over by Narses, acclaimed Belisarius. A bloodthirsty battle broke out between the two factions.

Under cover of the noisy fighting, the resourceful Mundus, with two hundred horsemen, entered the hippodrome by the Gate of Death, through which the bodies of gladiators killed in combat were carried out. From that moment, the rioters were beset on every side.

The guards had dismounted; climbing the tiers one by one, they massacred the insurgents. For hours they wielded their swords relentlessly.

Night fell on the hippodrome amid a tumult of sound: the joyful shouts of the victors mingled with the moans of the dying; the cold moonlight shone on the grey corpses of more than thirty thousand victims, whose mangled bodies lay in their last rest.

*   *   *

In the town the cry of "Victory!" had been succeeded by that of "Vengeance!" The Green supporters
were pursued and slaughtered everywhere. Tribonian,
Eudemon and Calopodios, who had resumed their posts,
were determined to repress the Nika rebellion harshly,
to provide a lesson for the future.

Anastasius' nephews were arrested and led before
Justinian. Pompeius was weeping miserably. Hypatius,
the stronger of the two, still protested his loyalty. He
claimed that though he had been placed, despite himself, at the head of the rebels, his only aim was to deliver
them up, defenceless, to the swords of the imperial
troops.

"Perhaps," replied Justinian. "But since you had
authority over these lunatics, you should have prevented
them from burning my city!"

The emperor was, nevertheless, disposed to be indul-
gent. But Theodora was watching at his side. She demanded that the guilty be punished:

"Compassion is a crime," said she, "when it is applied to the enemies of the State."

So Anastasius' nephews were executed; their bodies
were thrown into the Bosphorus and their possessions
confiscated. The repression also included senators,
magistrates and officials who had supported the rising,
if only briefly. Many were hanged or exiled.

The emperor ordered a proclamation to be read in
all the provinces, announcing his victory:

"God has enabled us to crush the miscreants," it
read. "It is our will to rebuild all that they burned
down in their mortal rage—above all, the church of St.

Sophia, which we desire to make into the largest and most beautiful church in Christendom."

Theodora, not content with punishing the leaders of the revolt, also tried to overthrow those who had shown lack of resolution at the crucial moment. She hated John of Cappadocia and demanded his dismissal. But Justinian refused to be deprived of a man who was so skilful at filling the coffers of the State, and who was a good adviser as well.

The empress rewarded the loyal commanders, Belisarius and Mundus, yet reproached them harshly for not having intervened sooner. Narses, on the other hand, was loaded with honours.

As for herself, because of the service she had rendered, Theodora now demanded an even more significant role in imperial affairs. From then on, at the side of a husband who adored her, she became in truth the all-powerful empress, the *Augusta*, chosen by God.

3

At the Sacred Palace

EAVING his sumptuous villa in Blachernai at dawn on April 15th, 538, Senator Probus embarked from the Golden Horn in a caïque painted in brilliant colours. At that early hour there were only a few other passengers: a black-robed monk from the monastery at Chora, a Syrian merchant, and two soldiers from the Lombard garrison which was encamped under the ramparts.

When he reached the port of Bucoleon, Senator Probus seated himself in a litter hung with purple silk. It was carried by black slaves who walked at a slow pace with its cedar poles inlaid with ivory resting on their shoulders. Guards went ahead, clearing a path through the crowd with their long, iron-tipped staves:

"Make way! Make way for the illustrious senator!"

Probus arrived at the Sacred Palace, the guards opened the bronze gates to him and he entered the vestibule, the Chalcé. Under the dome of the wide rotunda, coloured marbles and gilded mosaics mingled their luminous colours. This was where the imperial dignitaries gossiped together before entering the audience chambers and offices of the palace.

Probus did not linger in the Chalcé. He walked down a long gallery, on to which the halls of the emperor's guards and grooms opened. Soldiers in white tunics, holding lances, guarded the entrance to the private apartments and to the consistory, the great State room.

The senator left the gallery by a pink marble staircase and found himself once again in the warmth of the spring sunshine. Here, in a huge park, the buildings were arranged round tiled courtyards, linked by archways and gardens. Flower-beds, shaded by plane trees, fountains of clear water and pavilions with strange shapes inspired by Persia or distant India were blended into a harmonious design.

Probus spent a moment in meditation in a little chapel before an icon of St. Andrew, his patron. Then he entered a circular room with bare walls; it had an intimate atmosphere, conducive to work. There the emperor's advisers were seated at a round table: the quaestor Tribonian, John of Cappadocia—Prefect of the Praetorium, one or two senators, a lawyer, a judge: some fifteen people in all.

"Greetings to you, Probus," said Tribonian. "What news do you bring us from the city?"

"The town is calm," replied the senator, "and every-one is thankful that order and justice are well established there."

"Very good! That is because of our achievements in drawing up a single, clear code of laws for the whole empire, applying equally to everyone . . ."

Suddenly there was silence. The emperor appeared, preceded by two officers of his guard. He had a friendly word for everyone. Justinian was at that time a man of about forty, of medium height, with a round, ruddy face, curly brown hair already growing a little thin, a fine moustache and lively eyes. He had grown in confidence since defeating the circus factions, and nothing about him now recalled the panic-stricken sovereign of the time of the Nika rebellion.

Besides, Justinian considered himself the heir and guardian of the greatness of Rome. He was preceded by guards carrying the axe—originally carried by the Roman officers called lictors; he wore the white toga with a purple border which was the prerogative of the consuls, and he sat on a special seat, such as the Roman magistrates had used.

"I congratulate you," he said, "on having collected in one clear code, after years of work, all the laws and edicts published in the course of more than four centuries. Thanks to all of you, Roman law is embodied in one book, the *Digest*. Law students now have a fine work at their disposal, the *Institutes*. Finally, the *Novellae* which we are now writing will inform all the citizens of the empire of the laws they must observe."

"The code will bear your name, Justinian," said the

quaestor, "and it will be the great masterpiece of your reign."

Tribonian was a good courtier. He knew how to touch on a sensitive chord. The emperor grew enthusiastic:

"Justice is my aim. Power is nothing without law. Conquerors go down through history in a welter of blood and dust. Only legislators can found a State on a solid and lasting basis."

All morning the emperor worked with the lawyers, often acting as final arbiter.

"I maintain," stated Theophilus, a professor of law and a great traditionalist, "that the father of the family must have absolute power over his wife and children."

"And I," replied Probus, "believe that, for us, Roman severity should bow to the Christian spirit, which protects the weak both in the family and in the city."

Justinian, as a true believer, had no hesitation in supporting the senator:

"So be it, Probus! Continue to defend your ideas of justice here, for I have need of counsellors such as you."

*   *   *

In the early afternoon Probus was back in the Chalcé where the imperial dignitaries, drawn up in due order under the direction of the Master of the Palace, were preparing to walk in procession along the great gallery. They passed between a double line of guards, who formed a steel tunnel with their crossed lances, while the sound of cymbals and organs echoed round the hall. Servants hurried to draw back the silken hangings, disclosing at the end of the gallery the three ivory doors to the consistory.

The patriarch Epiphanus came forward, carrying the mitre and gold-embroidered pallium—or imperial cloak. With his cross he knocked on each of the doors, and they opened to reveal an immense and sumptuously decorated chamber. On the marble walls the light was reflected from panels of silver or silver-gilt decorated with emeralds, rubies and amethysts. The floor was of jasper and onyx, mingling in delicate whorls which blossomed into brilliant flowers.

At the end of the room two golden thrones encrusted with precious stones had been placed for the imperial couple on a porphyry dais, under a golden cupola supported by twisted columns, between two Victories with outspread wings, holding out laurel crowns.

The senators, bishops and generals took their places on one side of the room, with the empress's ladies-in-waiting facing them. These preparations did not take place in silence, but the great organs drowned the noise with their solemn peal, imparting an air of mysterious grandeur to the scene. There was silence as Justinian and Theodora appeared. The Master of the Palace spoke, and the assembled company took up the chant:

"Glory to you, all-powerful Caesar, good and merciful. Glory to you, divine Augusta. Long live our well-beloved sovereigns!"

Justinian seated himself on the throne. He was wearing a blue, gold-embroidered tunic with the purple pallium held on the shoulders by silver clasps. The ceremonial crown was on his head and he held in his hands the naked sword, representing force, and the gilt orb surmounted by a silver cross—the symbol of world sovereignty. Theodora was at his side, pale and very calm, wrapped in a cloak of violet brocade. The coils of her brown hair were held in place by fillets of pearls and encircled by a diadem scintillating with diamonds and rubies.

The Master of the Palace approached Justinian:

"The envoys of the Avars," he announced, "beg to be permitted to kneel at the feet of the emperor."

"Let them come in; I consent," replied Justinian. ·

The Avars had but recently left the cold steppes of the Danube basin. Arriving at the palace they were confronted by the guards in their white tunics and golden helmets with red plumes, carrying great shields engraved with the name of Christ, and long lances which seemed to flash like shafts of lightning. Now they were entering the huge consistory, filled with a crowd of impatient and curious courtiers.

"Look! There they are!" said the Byzantines.

But the Avars came to a sudden halt, as if struck dumb, at the threshold of the marble doors, dazzled by the light falling from the golden vault where angels and doves glided in brilliant mosaic.

"That is Targites!"

The spectators stared stonily at the Avar chieftain. So this was he, that Targites who had so often checked the violent onslaught of the Huns! There he stood, nervous and ill at ease. Then he made up his mind to advance, heavy-footed, his chest covered by a leather jerkin, his legs wrapped in cloth leggings, the hair

knotted on top of his head. Mounting the dais, he prostrated himself three times before the emperor, kissing
the red-slippered feet.

Justinian condescended to invite the Avar chieftain to
rise. He accepted his homage and the presents he had
brought: a heavy sword with chased hilt for the emperor,
and a bronze, enamelled coffer for Theodora.

Then the Master of the Palace read the imperial
decree:

"It has pleased us, Caesar of the Romans, to raise you,
Targites, chief of the Avars, to the rank of patrician, and
to accept your son as one of our shield-bearers. It will be
your duty to maintain three thousand horsemen on our
Danube frontiers and for this we shall pay you the sum
of ten thousand pieces of gold annually. We are confident that you will conduct yourself as a good and loyal
ally."

The text of the treaty was then translated into the
Avar language. It corresponded in every detail with the
pact which had been agreed after long negotiations:

"I swear by my gods to be a faithful ally," said
Targites.

Then Justinian called for a great rosewood chest, inlaid with mother-of-pearl, and displayed the contents
to the astonished Avars. What wonders it contained!
There were gold and silver urns, alabaster cups, ivory
carvings, fine pearls, bracelets set with amethysts and
sapphire flowers, amber and jade necklaces, and pieces
of gold, all cascading over the scarlet carpet:

"As you see," said the emperor, "we know how to reward our friends."

"And how to punish our enemies," added Theodora.

Before plunging their hands into the treasures before them, the Avars looked at Theodora—the slender, pale woman with her hard eyes and imperious voice. They thought of their own docile wives, subjected to the hardest toil and jolted from camp to camp in wagons, trembling at the first shout of their warriors. Targites spoke for them all when he admired Theodora:

"This woman," he said, "has the heart of a chieftain!"

*   *   *

As night was falling Probus arrived at the palace to attend the great official dinner given in honour of the Avars. For the senator, who was an elderly man, these interminable feasts were a real torture. But he feared to displease the emperor by failing to appear.

Probus was, in any case, opposed to all the favours bestowed on the Avars by Justinian. He expressed his views frankly to one of his friends, the historian Procopus:

"I do not trust these greedy barbarians. They serve us today because we shower them with gold, but they are quite ready to betray us tomorrow."

"No doubt," replied Procopus, "but they can fight, and when the Huns, the Bulgarians and the Persians are hurling themselves against the frontiers of the empire it is a good thing to have allies."

"Nevertheless, their fidelity is both costly and dubious."

Despite all this, Justinian had decided to welcome the Avars as friends. In an immense hall, known as the *triclinium*, more than two hundred guests took their places at nineteen tables, so arranged that no one had his back to the emperor. Under a ceiling panelled in purple and gold, great candelabra shed a diffuse light, while censers perfumed the air with myrrh and incense.

The servants had arranged dishes and goblets on marble tables covered with figured cloths. The jugglers and acrobats amused the guests, accompanied by the music of zithers and flutes. Along the walls fountains played, and their fresh streams sparkled on the iridescent marbles.

Probus had taken a seat between his friend Procopus and General Belisarius, with whom he hoped to discuss the coming expedition against the Persians. He knew the Persian people well and might have useful advice for the young commander. Then, at least, the dinner would not be a complete waste of time.

"Let the feasting begin!"

The Master of the Tables gave instructions to the servants, who darted in and out like dancers in a well-ordered ballet. Dish followed sumptuous dish: caviar from the Propontides, tunny from the Bosphorus, stuffed with honey, Thracian lamb roasted over a vine-wood fire, Phrygian goat in pepper sauce, Antioch pie dotted with grapes, rice cake full of preserved fruit, Armenian oranges and rose-petal jam, wine from Crete and the Cyclades . . .

Probus took little interest in the Avars, who were eating gluttonously. He was watching the imperial couple.

Justinian looked weary. He ate only a light meal: boiled beans, sheep's milk and a little honey. Theodora, on the other hand, stimulated and dominated the guests.

The empress tasted every dish, dismissing with a brusque gesture those she considered unworthy of her table. She demanded sophisticated food, perfectly presented. And, all the while, she entertained her guests by regaling them with well-chosen jests.

Probus was not fond of Theodora. Like everyone there, he knew that she was the daughter of a bear-leader, that she had led a dissolute life before marrying Justinian, and that she was hard, haughty and vindictive. But he admitted that, since the emperor's accession to the throne, she had shared all the burdens of power with her husband.

"That woman," said Belisarius, "was made to rule."

Probus agreed. That was exactly what Targites the Avar had said in the consistory. It was how people who met her usually reacted.

But the Avars had nothing to say now. They had eaten and drunk immoderately and, being unaccustomed to lavish meals, they had grown drowsy. Heads heavy, arms dangling, they cast uneasy glances at the soiled table, the empty flagons and the noisy guests, whom they could scarcely see through a thick mist. Then, their eyes completely dazzled by the splendours of Byzantium, they fell into a deep sleep.

4

Theodora the Imperious

IVELY in the cool of early morning, the crowds thronged in the arcades of the royal portico, where they loved to idle away the morning. There were orators, scribes, fashionable poets reciting their verses in front of the bookstalls. Further off, a ragged philosopher was discoursing learnedly on Plato and Aristotle, a hermit was telling of his solitary life in a desert cave, and a painter was displaying brightly-coloured pictures of saints. Astrologers, magicians and fortune-tellers offered to predict the future and the credulous and ever-anxious Byzantines eagerly discussed the omens and prophecies.

"What will tomorrow bring?" they asked one another with a shudder of superstitious fear.

This was the year 541 and so questions of topical

interest were also discussed: Belisarius' victories over the Persians, the misfortunes of Pope Silverius, the increased taxes imposed by the praetorian prefect, John of Cappadocia.

Justinian was popular. Since the Nika rebellion he had taken pains to regain his subjects' favour by brilliant conquests in Africa and Italy, great public works and sumptuous feasts where the Byzantines could give free rein to their taste for luxury and pleasure. But, above all, they were grateful to him for organising magnificent games, worthy of the new Rome. These were held at the hippodrome, which was no longer the scene of quarrels between the factions.

Theodora did not inspire the same affection. Women in particular loathed her, regarding her as an arrogant, cruel upstart.

"A circus girl," said one. "A street dancer on the throne of the Caesars! Scandalous!"

"And have you noticed the luxury and extravagance of her attire?" added another. "Nothing is exquisite enough for her. She would recoil from nothing, however infamous, to satisfy her least whim."

"Why does that surprise you?" asked a third. "She has complete control over her royal spouse; she made him drink one of those magic philtres; the magicians of the goddess Isis told her their secrets in Egypt. She is a creature of Satan, you may be sure!"

Men were less severe in their criticism. They were aware of the majestic beauty of the empress and of her charm when she wanted to please. But they did not accept her claim to rule the country, receive ambassadors and make and unmake ministers. Indeed, certain recent ignominious dismissals had given rise to great scandal.

"Did you see," muttered a well-known writer, "what happened to the patrician Germanus? He had the misfortune to anger the all-powerful Augusta. Although he was Justinian's nephew and an able general, he was exiled to a Phrygian village, where he lives by begging his bread."

"And the noble Theodosius?" added a professor of oratory. "Why does no one mention him any more? Because he is shut up in a subterranean dungeon. At the orders of the empress he is bound like a beast of burden in a stall and the chain is so short that he can neither stand up nor lie down. They say he has gone mad."

"Have you heard the news?"

Everyone pressed closer to the poet Agathias, for his inside knowledge of all the palace intrigues was unequalled. He spoke slowly, revealing his secret little by little.

"They say that Theodora intends to drive out the man who once called her 'circus girl' and who has earned her hatred. Yes, she has demanded the dismissal of John of Cappadocia!"

"Ah!" clamoured his audience. "For once we are in agreement with her, for that accursed Cappadocian is crushing us with taxes. Your news is too good to be true!"

At that moment, as the news was spreading through the crowd and the people were rejoicing over it, a procession reached the portico:

Next, a poor man in chains was thrust roughly forward

"Make way, make way!" shouted the guards, clearing a passage by laying about them with their cudgels. "Make way for the illustrious Prefect of the Praetorium!"

It was John himself, arrogant as ever. He was reclining comfortably in a rosewood litter with silken hangings. Robed in a green and gold tunic, adorned with jewels, elegant despite his girth, he was accompanied by pretty girls, who fanned and scented him and offered him wine to drink.

"Accursed tyrant," murmured the crowd, "is it possible that we shall soon be rid of you?"

But the prefect could afford to scorn the hatred he inspired. For ten years he had borne the heavy burden of the public finances. He would use any means in his power to fill the imperial coffers. In any case, his position depended on it.

So he entered the great hall of the praetorium, in which the plaintiffs were gathering. Poor wretches! They little knew what sort of reception awaited them.

The first to come forward was a peasant from a Thracian village; he stood awkwardly, bonnet in hand. He spoke on behalf of his village where the harvest had been pillaged by the Huns. He therefore begged for a reduction in the taxes, which he and his people were unable to pay.

"No," replied the prefect. "No question of it. Go and tell the people in your village that if they do not pay all they owe they will be sold as slaves."

A merchant from the harbour district was the next to speak. The guards had seized some silks and furs from

4

him without cause and he demanded the return of his property. When he was led away he started to protest, raising his voice.

"What?" said the Cappadocian. "Do you dare to oppose the government? You shall spend some time in prison to learn to keep your passions in check."

While the merchant was being dragged off another applicant approached. This was the prior of the monastery at Blachernai, carrying the mitre and silver cross of his office. He was indignant at the very heavy tax imposed on his abbey, which had the expensive task of providing hospitality and refuge for pilgrims, paupers and the sick.

"The Church is rich," said the prefect. "It can pay."

The prior insisted, invoking the privileges of his order and imperial protection. But the Cappadocian had an answer for everything.

"Are you not aware, my dear prior, that your monks go about speaking ill of the government? I ought to have them arrested and convicted as rebels. Now, you had better pay the tax, or else . . ."

The prior withdrew. Next, a poor man in chains was thrust roughly forward by the guards. He was thin and pale and could scarcely totter forward. The strokes of the lash had left ridges on his back. Who would have recognised in this ragged prisoner the patrician Boutzes, one of the richest landowners of the empire?

"All my goods are yours, my lord. I consent. I will do what you ask, I will give you everything, I will resist no longer. But, for pity's sake, let me see the light of day again."

"So you have been persuaded to change your attitude. Sign here that you renounce all your goods to the State."

"And what is to become of me?"

"Leave the city immediately and get yourself hanged elsewhere!"

The onlookers had tears in their eyes. This poor, broken man, tortured and despoiled by the brutal Cappadocian, had once been one of the finest generals of the empire. But why did Justinian continue to trust a minister whom everyone loathed?

*   *   *

It was true that Theodora had decided to drive out the Prefect of the Praetorium. She had long detested him and was still bitter because he had once been a friend to the Greens, because he had counselled flight at the time of the Nika rebellion and because he indulged his taste for comfort and pleasure at Court. She had never forgotten the contemptuous words he had used about her and which had at once been reported to her: "circus girl" or even "bear-leader". In any case, surely the downfall of the hated prefect would make the people fonder of their empress?

Theodora had several times asked Justinian to dismiss the Cappadocian:

"He is a greedy, corrupt, cruel man. The people would bless you if you dismissed him. Moreover, he is an impious man, who laughs at sacred things. Finally, he is ambitious, his fortune is immense and the men he takes into his service would do anything to put the empire in his hands. How can you, Caesar, continue to tolerate in your palace a rival who desires nothing but your ruin!"

Justinian listened, knowing that there was some truth in Theodora's harsh criticism. But he had no desire to lose an active, energetic minister who was skilled at filling the State coffers.

"A sovereign," he replied simply, "can do nothing great unless he is well financed. John provides me with money, and I need him. If he were plotting against me I would break him without remorse, but I cannot believe that he is."

Furious because she had failed to convert Justinian to her views, Theodora thought of having her enemy assassinated by her own men. But he was well guarded and, having learned of the empress's plans through his spies, he redoubled his precautions. He would say to anyone who would listen:

"I am not a Paschal lamb ready for the slaughter."

Nevertheless, he was worried; in order to find out what fate had in store for him, he went to Hermidas the soothsayer. There, in an almost inaccessible cave haunted by bats, the soothsayer consulted rolls of papyrus covered with strange symbols. In the flickering light of an oil lamp, he handed the tensely expectant prefect a sheet on which certain words were inscribed. This was the expected oracle, enigmatically worded as usual:

"You will soon be wearing the robe of Augustus."

John of Cappadocia read and re-read it several times, and his heart was filled with joy. The robe of Augustus? That must undoubtedly be the imperial mantle. Soon, then, for the oracle was clear, his supreme desire to ascend the throne would be fulfilled. And, after all, what was surprising about that? The Emperor Justinian had been nothing but an ignorant soldier when he was crowned. Why should he, a patrician, a consul, the Prefect of the Praetorium, not take the place of Justinian, who had become a plaything in the hands of a circus girl?

When he was emperor it would be his first business to take vengeance on Theodora, who had recently—he had proof of it—paid some of her slaves to insinuate themselves into the Palace of the Praetorium and put poison in his food . . .

*   *   *

Assured now of his future, John of Cappadocia made a grand tour of the East. Wherever he went he confiscated the goods of the rich and distributed gold to the petty chiefs and soldiers to win their support. He obtained formal promises from them to join in a march on Byzantium. From day to day he felt that he was drawing nearer to the throne.

But Theodora was keeping watch. Belisarius, the most distinguished general of the army of the East, had taken to wife the lovely Antonina, who was an intimate friend of the empress. Antonina was the daughter of a charioteer at the hippodrome and had often helped Theodora to carry out her subtle intrigues. Beautiful, intelligent, well versed in the secrets of the court, she was both confidante and accomplice to her sovereign, whom she adored:

"You know that the Cappadocian is in the East,"

Theodora said to her one day, "and that he is plotting to seize the throne. If, by misfortune, he should succeed, his first act would be to put Belisarius to death, for he is jealous of his fame. And you would share your husband's fate."

"I hate the Cappadocian." replied Antonina. "If I can help you to punish this man's insolence I will do it gladly."

"Listen well, then. This is my plan . . ."

A few days later Antonina went to the public baths. There she met, according to plan, the only daughter of the Prefect of the Praetorium, the gentle and naïve Euphemia. She was a girl of about fifteen, who had been very lonely since her father's departure. The subtle Antonina found it easy to gain her friendship, entertaining and flattering the child who was in need of affection.

From then on they were inseparable. They went about the city together, buying beautiful materials, jewels and perfume. They laughed uproariously at the mimes and jugglers. They went for a trip on the Golden Horn in a caïque, its brown sails filled by the wind, to admire the reflection of the sun on the battlemented city. They went together, bearing their tapers, to kiss the revered relics in the church of the Holy Apostles. Euphemia felt free and happy. . . .

One evening when they were alone, Antonia confided in her young friend. She complained bitterly that her husband Belisarius had been poorly rewarded for his victories in Africa and Italy. Suddenly recalled to Constantinople, the general had been ignored and left for almost a year without a command. He had been remembered when the war against the Persians began, but even then he had been given a weak and poorly equipped army.

"But why?" asked the girl. "Is he not the best general in the empire?"

"Yes, but Theodora hates him."

Day after day Antonina complained of the empress who, she said, insulted her in public and maltreated her. One night she took refuge with Euphemia, for the empress (in order to give credence to the tale) had actually driven Antonina out of the palace. People were talking of nothing but the shocking humiliation of Belisarius' wife. Euphemia therefore felt no suspicion. Since she herself loathed Theodora, she asked Antonina:

"But why does Belisarius, who has devoted soldiers under his command, bear with all these injustices? Why does he not revolt?"

"The truth is," replied Antonia, "that one can do nothing with an army unless one has an ally in the capital. Oh, if only your father would join us, everything would be easy. But I am well aware that he is not very fond of Belisarius."

Soon afterwards, on returning from his triumphal journey in the East, John of Cappadocia was joyfully reunited with his daughter. She at once reported to him the conversations she had had with Antonina. He was delighted. Had the longed-for opportunity to don "the mantle of Augustus" come at last?

Belisarius was regarded as loyal to Justinian, but it was true that he had good reason for resentment against the imperial couple, who had often treated him unjustly.

Moreover, everyone knew that Belisarius was totally subject to his wife's will; if Antonina asked him to act, he would do so. And it would make all the difference to the success of the revolt if Belisarius were involved in the plot!

So the prefect told his daughter to inform Antonina that he wanted a secret meeting with her. Trembling with joy, Euphemia ran to her friend:

"My father thinks," she said, "that there is not a moment to lose."

But Antonia refused. She said that great caution was needed, for Theodora's spies were everywhere. She had another suggestion to make, however:

"In a few days I am going to join Belisarius with the army of the East. I shall spend the night on the way in one of our villas at Rufinianes, not far from the city. Tell your father to join me there, where we can talk freely. I shall try to obtain my husband's full support for the affair we have discussed together."

Euphemia took the reply to her father. The prefect approved this discreet meeting. Yes, caution was necessary. He would go to the rendezvous and he himself would take every possible precaution. Antonina hastened to announce the news to Theodora. The trap was laid and ready to be sprung . . .

*   *   *

The empress had been in touch with General Narses and with Marcellus, the Captain of the Guard. They would go to Rufinianes, hide themselves in the garden of the villa and, as soon as treason was mentioned, they would seize the prefect, dead or alive.

Justinian had agreed. He did not want to believe that his ablest supporter could be at the centre of a plot. His conscience at least would be clear. But might this not be some treacherous ruse of Theodora's? He knew his wife well, knew her to be arrogant and vindictive. He called one of his officials and murmured to him:

"Tell John of Cappadocia from the emperor that he must not leave the city on any pretext, for his life is in danger. Do you understand?"

But the prefect ignored this warning. He had no use for the advice of Justinian, whose place he would soon be taking as Head of State. He simply decided to take a few soldiers with him as a bodyguard.

Night came. The scent of flowers hung heavily on the air. The villa overlooking the sea stood out among the deep shadows. In the park surrounding it all was quiet. The only sound that could be heard was the faint whisper of the waves and the rustling of the great pines in the gentle breeze. Antonina arrived punctually for the meeting, at an hour auspicious for plots and secrets.

"I have come in answer to your summons," said the prefect. "It seems that I may be useful to you."

"Belisarius is ready to act, he is only waiting for your support."

"Has he made up his mind to depose Justinian?"

"Yes."

"Then he can count on me."

At these words Narses and Marcellus, who were hidden in the bushes nearby, sprang up and attempted to seize the prefect, while Antonina, playing the scene she had rehearsed to perfection, screamed:

"Alas! We are betrayed!"

Hearing the noise, John's guards rushed up, and a fight began. Marcellus was wounded, but he urged on his own men.

"We have him! Kill him if he resists!"

Narses, sword in hand, ran forward, crying:

"Yield, Cappadocian! We will make you pay for all your crimes."

But the prefect managed to escape under the cover of darkness. Running down to the shore, he found a fishing-boat; tugging desperately at the oars, he reached the city. What was he to do? He took refuge in the church of St. Sophia, where he invoked the right of sanctuary. Did he remember that when he himself was pursuing one of his victims he had often defied that sacred right?

Theodora, whom Narses had informed of the situation, went to Justinian and told him the story. She brought witnesses and demanded that the prefect be disgraced, as a first step. The emperor was forced to yield. The news ran through the town, causing great joy. Small matter how it had been done: the Cappadocian had been driven out at last, and would be punished.

The order was given for his arrest and there was up-roar in St. Sophia. He was seized, tonsured and summarily clothed in the robe of a monk who had just died. This monk had been called—Augustus. And so—but in a very different sense from that which the prefect had expected—the mysterious prophecy of Hermidas was fulfilled.

Justinian soon learned of Theodora's part in the affair. And he was far from pleased. He decided to show clemency. John of Cappadocia, who had gone astray temporarily, but whose good and loyal services had long been valued, was allowed to keep part of his possessions and to leave for Cyzicus on the Asian coast. Once there, he would have resigned himself to a peaceful retirement had Theodora not pursued him with her passionate hatred.

First she had him charged in connection with the murder of a bishop; he was arrested, imprisoned and beaten. Then she had him exiled to Egypt, where he had to live as a beggar, without any means of his own. Finally, she sent men to kill him. He escaped them, but was reduced to a life of misery and terror.

But his spirit was not broken. He bore all these trials with courage, giving advice to men of finance and even amusing himself by reminding the citizens of Alexandria of the sum they owed to the treasury. When Theodora had gone, he returned to Byzantium.

In the city which had once trembled at his feet, no one knew him. He offered his services to Justinian, who refused—in memory of Theodora. So he retired to the church of St. Sophia. There, the former unbeliever astonished his brothers by his piety. He died of old age, forgotten by everyone, in the homespun robe which he had assumed one day despite himself: the robe of a monk called Augustus.

A similar but unjust fate was to befall Belisarius.

5

Belisarius

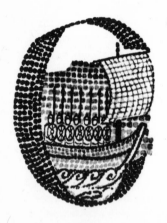

ONSTANTINOPLE was enjoying a holiday, for it was June 22nd, 533 and the fleet was fitting out for Africa. More than six hundred ships had left the Golden Horn early that morning and were now passing in procession before the imperial port of Bucoleon. In their orderly ranks were the *chelandia*—heavy vessels with several banks of oars which were used to transport troops—and a whole concourse of fast, narrow ships which were to protect the convoy.

The people clustered on the quays, glorying in the greatness of Byzantium. Justinian and Theodora were there, beneath a canopy of purple and gold, surrounded by the Court and the people. Everyone was watching the scene on the water: the great vessels with their carved prows, their tapering keels and their wide sails swelling in the wind.

"May God protect our army!"

That was the cry as the troop transports passed, with the helmeted soldiers lined up in impeccable order on their decks, spear in hand, oval shields overlapping one another like glittering scales.

In time Belisarius' own ship passed. Its mainmast carried the sacred gold and azure banner depicting the Mother of God. The young general, in his red cloak, saluted the imperial couple with his naked sword. The shouts of the crowd redoubled, for everyone admired this tall commander with his fine features and black beard, his lively and steadfast eyes.

"I trust Belisarius," the emperor declared to his court. "He is the only man who can make a success of this difficult enterprise."

Theodora said nothing. She had no liking for Belisarius, despite the invaluable help he had given her at the time of the Nika rebellion. She feared his ambition. After all, she thought, it was not a bad thing for him to be away from Byzantium on a risky expedition.

The plan to reconquer Africa—now in the hands of the Vandals—although it had delighted the emperor, was such a bold one that the ministers had heard it with amazement. The praetorian prefect, John of Cappadocia, had opposed it with all the means in his power.

"This is madness!" he had said. "The Persians, the Huns and the Bulgarians are all threatening our frontiers, the treasury is empty, the army is exhausted, and now we are to embark on a perilous war against a prince who wants to be our friend!"

But Justinian would not listen. It was his intention to

wrest from the power of the barbarians those countries of the former Roman empire which they had no right to occupy. Above all, he wanted the rich lands of Africa.

"The Emperor of Rome cannot renounce Carthage!"

So the fleet left Constantinople, sailed down the Asian coast and headed for Greece and Sicily. There, at the foot of Mount Etna, the men took some rest. They were well received by their ally, the Governor of the Goths, who detested the Vandals. Belisarius had no difficulty in obtaining water, food and horses here. Above all, he was able to discover what was happening in the enemy kingdom:

"King Gelimer, we are told, is not expecting an attack. He recently sent his brother Tzazo and the whole of his fleet against Sardinia, where a revolt has broken out. He himself is fighting with his army along the borders of the desert against the Moors. He is four days' march from the coast."

Belisarius set sail at once and disembarked with eight thousand horsemen and ten thousand foot-soldiers on the African coast, without meeting any opposition. The wind had carried him southward and he calculated that he would need a week to reach Carthage. So they marched cautiously along the shore, where they were within reach of the fleet in case they needed protection.

Belisarius was counting on the support of the local inhabitants who were loyal to the memory of the great empire. He had given very strict orders to his troops:

"We are in a Christian country here, a province of the

empire. I will not tolerate any pillaging or violence. God is my witness that we have come to liberate our brothers and not to oppress them."

The news spread quickly, and the people gathered confidently to welcome Belisarius' soldiers and bring them food. The towns opened their gates.

Informed of the danger, King Gelimer returned with all speed to try to block the road to Carthage against the Byzantines. He occupied a rocky gorge which seemed to offer him a secure position. But at the first assault his troops fled in disorder. Discouraged, the king observed:

"The Vandals have lost their valour; they have no heart for battle now."

So Belisarius entered Carthage and rebuilt its ramparts. Gradually, he imposed his rule over the greater part of the country. At last he decided to complete his rout of the Vandals. He had heard that the enemy was encamped less than one day's march away. Leaving his infantry in the rear, he took his cavalry to the great plain, where the wind was stirring up dust devils and the sun struck down with its fiery fist.

The Vandals had made their camp on a height by the side of a small stream, swollen by the winter rains. Belisarius, as soon as he saw them, reined in his foam-flecked black charger and drew up his well-armed troops in order of battle. Would the Vandals take flight? Or would they attack in strength, with the courage of despair? They did neither, but stood calm and resolute, awaiting the assault.

Belisarius tried in vain to draw them into open country. Gelimer had explained to his men that their fate would be decided by this battle alone. He had reminded them that they were the heirs of that great people who had once left the dark forests of Germany, crossed Gaul and Spain and come at last to sunny Africa, leaving a memory of horror behind them wherever they went. The Vandals had sworn to stand firm under the attack.

Belisarius felt the growing impatience of his troops. He ordered the trumpets to be sounded and the standards raised. His horsemen crossed the stream and unleashed a hail of arrows upon the Vandals who were poorly protected by their round shields and leather tunics. The caparisoned chargers of the Byzantines bounded forward; their riders' bronze breastplates and crested helmets sparkled in defiance of the dust-laden air. Belisarius, spear in hand, fought in the front rank.

For hours, the Vandals stood firm; their deep ranks, bristling with pikes, repulsed the Byzantines towards the water. But the Byzantines returned again and again to the charge and in the clash of arms, with shouts and tumult, they penetrated the very heart of the enemy camp. Men and beasts rolled forward like clouds in a stormy sky, shot with the lightning of the lances . . .

The Vandals gave way step by step. Was this the end? No, not yet. Gelimer's brother Tzazo flung himself into the battle with his horsemen close behind him. He was bare-chested; his long hair hung loose down to his shoulders; he wielded a heavy axe in his two hands. The exhausted Byzantines fell back to recover their breath.

In the confusion of the battle, which surged to and fro

like the tide, Belisarius had remained cool. He had kept back his *foederati*—the light cavalry composed of daring but unreliable horsemen who had come from the steppes of the Danube to serve the empire for gold. The lure of rich booty spurred the mercenaries to complete the rout of the Vandals. Tzazo was killed. Gelimer fled.

Some of the Vandal warriors, drawn up in square formation, continued to resist. The Byzantine infantry, which had reached the scene of battle by forced marches, riddled them with arrows and javelins. By sunset it was all over.

In their disarray the Vandals had abandoned their camp, leaving their treasures, weapons, food and even their wives and children, cooped up in the heavy wagons. Belisarius could not restrain his men; they now rushed to pillage the camp, despoiling the enemy corpses of their bracelets and gold collars and sharing out a vast booty among themselves.

Night fell suddenly. While a fresh breeze brought the smell of the sea to the devastated camp, all around it fires sprang up like stars. In the land of St. Augustine, the Byzantine army sang hymns of victory before going to sleep on the dewy earth. The Vandal kingdom had been swallowed up in one day, like rain in the desert sand.

* * *

Ten years had passed. Belisarius was in gloomy attendance at the palace among a crowd of courtiers. He felt ill at ease in this atmosphere of intrigue, where everyone was interested only in ministerial rivalries, quarrels of the hippodrome and religious disputes. The high dignitaries greeted him with cold courtesy and as he passed them murmured:

"Poor Belisarius! He cannot get over the loss of the imperial favour."

For, as everyone at court well knew, Justinian was now jealous of Belisarius' laurels. Theodora, the friend of his wife the beautiful Antonina, still felt nothing but dislike and contempt for the general. The nobles were pleased by his fall from favour. They now flattered the rising generals: Narses, Martin and Phocas. Only the people cheered Belisarius, for they did not forget what Byzantium owed to him.

For ten years Belisarius had been the principal architect of imperial glory. He had conquered Africa and offered Justinian the immense treasure of the Vandals. He had occupied Sardinia, Corsica and Sicily. He had landed in Italy, taken Naples by surprise, driven from Rome the Goths who had been watering their horses in the Tiber for a century. Finally, he had taken Ravenna, that great city where King Theodoric had erected battlements, palaces and the beautiful churches of St. Vital and St. Apollinarius, decorated with mosaics patiently assembled by artists from Byzantium.

Brave and loyal as he was, he had even succeeded in gaining the affection of those he had conquered. The Goths, worried by the Frankish threat, had asked him to become their king. He had refused:

"There is only one prince worthy to rule the world. That is the Roman emperor, the elect of God."

Yet Justinian felt no gratitude to Belisarius for his brilliant conquests. He had recalled him suddenly to

Byzantium and refused to grant him a triumph. Then, in order to be rid of him, he had sent him to fight the Persians with a ludicrously small army.

"This time at least," thought Theodora, "our fine hero will be defeated."

Not so. Plague ravaged the Persian camp. King Chosroes fled and, once again, Belisarius returned to Constantinople as the victor. The emperor hastily awarded him the title of Constable—a purely honorary office—vowing never again to give him a command.

"We will let him languish in prolonged retirement," said Theodora.

But Belisarius was not resigned. Day after day he wandered through the great rooms of the palace asking for an audience, which was always refused. The courtiers had become accustomed to seeing him. A few pitied him but most passed by, indifferent or sneering.

But one day a guard summoned Belisarius. Could it be true? Justinian wanted to see him immediately:

"Our affairs are going badly in Italy," grumbled the emperor. "The Goths have taken Naples and their chief, Totila, is threatening Rome. Would you like to make war on them?"

Belisarius accepted joyfully. But Justinian laid down conditions: the general could not take his bucellarians with him, for they must be left to protect Constantinople in case the Slavs or Persians attacked. He must recruit mercenaries where he could, at his own expense. Furthermore, he would have no authority over the other Byzantine commanders in Italy.

Belisarius did not argue, so eager was he to return to

the life of a soldier. But as soon as he arrived in Ravenna he had to think again. His troops were weak and poorly equipped. The Byzantine generals refused to help him.

Totila took advantage of this situation to seize Rome. Belisarius was reduced to begging the barbarian chief not to destroy the Eternal City.

"If I do not," Totila informed him, "it is only out of regard for you!"

Soon afterwards Belisarius learned that the Goths had set off for the south to pillage wealthy Sicily. He decided to risk everything in an attempt to reconquer Rome.

With a thousand horsemen, he made for the outskirts of the city. The ramparts were intact, but no one guarded them. The Goths of the garrison were established in the countryside on the banks of the Tiber. Belisarius hastily assembled his flat-bottomed boats to row up-river. He loaded them with soldiers, supplies and weapons.

One spring night, when the scent of thyme and mint were in the air and a gentle breeze brushed across the water meadows, the long barges glided off with a creak of oars. Soon, the Byzantines were close to the ruins; with just two strokes of their oars they could reach the spot from which the Goths were guarding the entrance to the city.

First, Belisarius gave orders for the breaking of the heavy chain which barred their passage up the river. Then he ordered his archers to fire arrows tipped with burning tow. Taken by surprise, the Goths fled while the barges passed beneath the wooden arches where flames were beginning to spring up, giving off clouds of smoke laced with sparks.

The Byzantine troops entered the deserted city which loomed up out of the shadows in the light of a pallid moon. They were greeted in the Forum by silent statues and abandoned sanctuaries. . . .

Belisarius spent a moment in contemplation in the midst of this dead city which had been the cradle of the empire, but his spirits soon revived. Preparations must be made to defend Rome. The walls were strengthened, the moats deepened, the towers and ramparts lined with engines of war—catapults, ballistae and slings. Reinforcements were summoned from all the Byzantine garrisons of Italy.

When Totila heard that Belisarius had taken Rome, he returned to the city with all speed and flung his weary horsemen into the assault. The Goths' attack was easily broken. Totila raised the siege and fled to the great northern plain, where he intended to recover his strength.

Belisarius, elated by his victory, sent his wife Antonina to Constantinople to ask for fresh troops and in particular for his valiant bucellarians. He hoped that Theodora would yield to her friend's entreaties. But Theodora had just died. Justinian, bitter and suspicious, listened once more to the slander of the courtiers who described Belisarius to him as an adventurer, prepared to take any step to rule the empire. The general was relieved of his command, recalled to Byzantium and accused of exceeding his authority. Nevertheless, thanks to his past services he was spared imprisonment . . .

*   *   *

Twelve years later . . . The crowd thronged the basilica of St. Sophia, where the patriarch, surrounded by bishops, was celebrating a solemn mass. An old man in a purple robe knelt near the altar, absorbed in his prayers. It was the Emperor Justinian.

The church, dedicated to Divine Wisdom, had never been more beautiful, with its brilliant mosaics on a gold background, and its green marble and porphyry columns, their capitals decorated with palms and acanthus leaves. The light from the ornamented candelabra sparkled on the ivory statues, the jewelled reliquaries, the hangings of brocade and damask. Incense burned in silver censers; and solemn organ music filled the huge nave, while choirs intoned the hymn of praise:

"Praise be to God, Light and Truth . . ."

Suddenly, the emperor raised his eyes to the high dome which seemed to be suspended from heaven on a golden chain. He was well content, for the huge dome was now perfectly safe. A young architect named Isidore had undertaken to reconstruct it after its collapse in the year 558, and he had succeeded. This second consecration of the basilica (in 563) would be the real one.

Justinian admired the great vault above him which was decorated with mosaics. There, against a blue sky in which golden angels soared and stars twinkled, Christ reigned in majesty, clad in a splendid robe, his countenance calm and stern, with the Mother of God at his side, very simple in her mourning veils—a woman of the people whose goodness showed in her tender eyes.

At the end of the ceremony the patriarch accompanied the emperor to the door of the church, where a great crowd had gathered. True to tradition, the beggars were in the front row holding out their bowls. A priest from the imperial chapel had the task of giving each a piece of silver so that they too might share in the general rejoicing.

Among them was a poor blind man with bare feet; his thin back was bowed and his head trembled. His clothes were shabby and he wore a battered helmet. His feeble voice murmured almost inaudibly:

"Alms, I beg you, for the unfortunate Belisarius!"

Justinian passed through the crowd of beggars very quickly, with an air of irritation. He did not notice the ragged beggar who had once been the greatest general of his reign: the once powerful Belisarius whom he, in his petty jealousy, had persecuted, caused to be arrested on a charge of conspiracy and blinded in a dungeon, before being flung out into the gutter.

"Listen to the story of poor Belisarius . . ."

The blind man was talking. He spoke of the Persians, the Vandals, the Goths and the Huns. He repeated the words which clamoured in his brain: battle, victory, triumph. He said that he had been a patrician and a consul, that medals had been struck in his honour. But no one paid any attention to the words of the deranged old man. Only a few children walked alongside him, mischievously tapping on his helmet and grabbing at his stick.

All through the town, an oblivious crowd was preparing to celebrate the glory of Justinian.

"Listen to the story of poor Belisarius . . ."

But no one heeded the mournful plea.

6

Ambitious Irene

When Kings Marry Shepherdesses . . .

N bygone days there lived a very beautiful and mighty sovereign. She was a widow and she reigned over the most splendid empire in the world. When her son, the heir to the throne, was seventeen years old she tried to find a suitable wife for him. She was looking for a young girl who was perfect in every particular, and she sent envoys to every province of her realm in search of this girl. . . .

This story begins like a fairy tale, yet it is the true account of the marriage of Constantine, son of Irene, Empress of Byzantium.

Irene, a young Athenian of great beauty, had caught the attention of the Basileus, Leo IV, who had married her in the year 768 and then shared his throne with her. But twelve years later Leo IV died. As Constantine was still only a child, he was left in peace to play at knuckle-bones in the gardens and to study Greek under the guidance of illustrious teachers, while the Empress Irene governed the empire. It was a heavy burden for the young queen, who had to unravel intrigues, foil plots and defend the throne against usurpers. Even those nearest to her conspired against her. But Irene fought on stubbornly. "It is my duty," she said, "to preserve the throne for my son Constantine. May God give me the strength to succeed!"

Once gentle, she now became hard, violent and deceitful, as she had to be in that cruel Byzantine world which she must control.

Constantine grew up at her side, full of admiration for his mother. He was a docile and grateful child. Although he preceded her in the glittering procession which attended the services at St. Sophia on holy days, and although, as his rank demanded, he was the first to receive the applause of the crowd cheering its rulers at the hippodrome, yet he was glad to leave the government of the empire in Irene's firm hands.

When the prince was of an age to take a wife his mother declared:

"I want none of these politically arranged marriages for my son. I want him to be happy; that is why I desire for him, above all, a young girl as wise as she is beautiful, adorned with every grace of heart and mind. What do riches matter! Was not the great Theodora a poor girl when Justinian raised her to the supreme rank?"

But, the exercise of power had made Irene extremely methodical; she resolved to leave nothing to chance.

Messengers scoured the empire, preceded by heralds in embroidered tunics sounding their trumpets. Every town, every village was visited; and this took many months. When a crowd, drawn by the noise and magnificence of the procession, had gathered round the court envoys, a parchment roll bearing the imperial seal was unrolled. The messenger read out what was written on it and then, after a copy had been nailed up in the square, the procession passed on, leaving behind a crowd of people who discussed the matter eagerly, exclaiming and commenting for days on the official decree.

What were the contents of this proclamation which so astonished Irene's subjects?

It gave exact details of the height, weight and figure required of Constantine's future wife. Irene demanded a particular type of face, rejected certain colours for eyes or hair, and laid down the ideal proportions. She even stipulated the size—a very small one—of her future daughter-in-law's feet.

All the girls who fulfilled these conditions were to present themselves at the palace. Irene and Constantine would receive the candidates, talking to each of them in order to assess their qualities of heart and mind. Finally, after thorough examination, the name of the chosen girl would be proclaimed.

*   *   *

While the imperial emissaries were thus making their long journey through the provinces, they arrived one evening at a manor house of impressive size, outlined against the evening sky. It was in Paphlagonia; the day had been arduous, the going rough and the sun relentless. Both men and beasts were exhausted and parched with thirst. They decided to ask lodging for the night from the master of the house. The imperial standard would be a good enough recommendation: they were certain to be received hospitably.

Their welcome was indeed a warm one, but the man who came to meet the travellers certainly did not have the outward appearance of a wealthy lord. Although his manners were gracious, his poor and shabby clothing might have led them to mistake him for a peasant. He led his guests into an almost empty hall. There were no soft carpets on the worn tiles and no hangings on the bare stone walls. The furniture consisted of nothing more than a great table of rough wood and a few rustic stools. How far the courtiers had travelled from the splendours of the Sacred Palace!

Philaretus, the master of the house, gave a cheerful hail, and a moment later a woman entered. She had an air of great dignity but she too was dressed very humbly. Her face showed signs of deep distress when her husband told her:

"Here are our guests. As a faithful subject of our revered empress I wish to offer them the best possible hospitality. Let us have a good dinner; roast some fowl."

While the travellers chatted among themselves and washed the grime from their faces and hands in the fresh water which was brought to them, the woman drew her husband into a corner of the room and spoke to him in an undertone:

"What am I to do? I have nothing to roast—no beef, no tender lambs, no fowls. You have distributed all your goods to the poor; of course, I do not reproach you for this, for you were following the teaching of Our Lord and everyone says that you are a holy man. But how can I honour our guests with a dinner worthy of them? They cannot be content as we are with beans and butter and cheese; I would die of shame to serve them such modest fare!"

"Why do you worry? God will provide. Do you lack faith? Light your fire and trust in Him."

Then Philaretus returned to his guests and invited them to sit down on the wooden stools, with as little awkwardness as if he had been offering them sumptuous couches. Then he began to talk to them while his wife blew until she was breathless on a fire of green wood which produced more smoke than flame.

Suddenly, joyful shouts echoed round the courtyard and three young men burst into the hall; they stopped dead when they saw the grandly dressed visitors, looking so out-of-place in that austere setting. Then they came forward. They were Philaretus' grandsons and their grandfather introduced them to the imperial messengers. They were strong, merry lads—although their clothes were almost in rags—and very excited by their adventures. Not only had they brought back a basketful of eels caught in the nets they had laid in the nearby river, but they were also very proud of having shot with their slings three pheasants which had come to drink from the fresh water.

"Does God ever desert those who put their trust in Him?" asked the master of the house simply.

The meal was delicious, served in humble earthen-ware vessels, certainly, but by the gracious hands of young Mary, Philaretus' grand-daughter. She was charming and, despite her patched grey woollen dress, the palace emissaries were struck by her beauty. They saw at once that she corresponded in every particular to the imperial specifications.

So, not without difficulty, they persuaded Philaretus and his wife to accompany their grand-daughter to Constantinople so that she might compete for the crown. They had decided, in gratitude for the hospitality they had received, to pay the expenses of this long journey themselves, since it was too costly for such poor folk.

*   *   *

A large number of girls had arrived at the palace since the imperial edict had been proclaimed. Many had been sent back almost at once. At last only twelve candidates were left. The empress had long conversations with these twelve young beauties; she invited them to eat with her and took them for walks in order to get to know them better; but she had never let fall a hint of her intentions.

At last, the great day arrived when Irene and Constantine were to announce their choice officially. The girls awaited the verdict in a state of great excitement. Which of them was to be empress? All deserved the title by virtue of their beauty, and the colourful group was like a charming bouquet whose brilliance exceeded that of the baskets of flowers which surrounded them. Among them was Mary of Amnia, little Mary who had formerly worn such poor drab clothes and was now dressed in embroidered silks. She spoke to the others:

"Sisters, we have no idea which of us is to be raised to the supreme rank. The chosen one will be all-powerful from this day on. Therefore I suggest that we make a pledge to one another: if God grants that one of us is to reign, that one shall undertake not to forget her eleven friends, and to have regard for their welfare!"

Most of the other girls agreed, but one who had been playing idly with her golden bracelets, pretending not to be interested in the conversation, intervened haughtily:

"It would not be charitable for me to leave you in doubt any longer. Do you not understand that the emperor's choice is already made? No doubt you all have some grace and wit, but you are of low birth, your manners are awkward, you would be ill at ease upon the throne. I, on the other hand, am noble, my father is a strategus and he is rich and well received at court. And, as to beauty, let me say without boasting that I have no fear of competition from any one of you."

The girl who spoke was fair-haired; her bearing was arrogant and her eyes commanding. She did indeed seem made to rule; her eleven companions were already resigned to defeat. She added lightly:

"But have no fear, I shall take good care not to forget you. . . ."

She walked away, her long green gown with its deep pleats swaying gracefully.

Who would have believed it? Irene, so imperial, so dominant, did not choose a daughter-in-law with the same qualities as she herself possessed.

"My child," she said to the daughter of the strategus,

"you have been blessed with every gift, yet I do not think that you would be a good wife for the emperor."

And her choice and that of Constantine, who agreed with his mother in everything, fell upon the humble Mary, the little Paphlagonian who would never have dared to dream of such an honour.

Thus it was that the Basileus Constantine, son of the Empress Irene, married Mary, one of the poorest girls of his realm, but also the most beautiful and virtuous.

Sad Ending to a Fairy Tale

When the last echoes of the marriage ceremonies had died away and the new Augusta had been installed at the Sacred Palace, Irene realised that she would find it difficult to tolerate the presence of the young empress.

She had deliberately chosen a girl of poor background in order to be sure of the gratitude of the girl whom she had thus honoured; she had wanted her to be gentle and timid so that she could control her the better. Even Mary's beauty was to have been a weapon for Irene.

"My daughter-in-law," she thought, "will rule the heart of the emperor, who will be unable to refuse anything to his beloved wife. She, for her part, will be entirely devoted to me and will follow my instructions. Thus, through her, I shall continue to govern the empire, as it is right and natural that I should."

So Irene's choice, apparently disinterested, had in fact been dictated by her ambition and her thirst for power.

Yet, although Mary had exactly the qualities expected

of her, Irene was worried. The cheers which the crowd meted out ungrudgingly to Mary's youth and beauty were like wounds to the pride of the old empress.

Moreover, Constantine was growing more independent and more decided. Was he growing away from her? This boy whom she had kept in childhood so long was becoming a man, a man who would one day refuse to share his throne—even with his mother, once so greatly admired:

"Yet he owes everything to me!" thought Irene bitterly.

For his part the young emperor did not seem quite as delighted with his beautiful companion as Irene had expected. He very quickly lost interest in her and even seemed to display a certain distaste for her, as if he found it difficult to bear the idea that she had been chosen by his mother. Was he doomed to depend on Irene in everything, even in the choice of a wife?

The courtiers around him were eager to do his bidding, his zealous servants were attentive to his slightest whim. But Constantine told himself morosely that in the midst of his brilliant Court and despite the flattery which surrounded him, he had no more authority, was no more the ruler, than the docile child of former years, sometimes invited to greet the crowd at the empress's side, and then sent back to his apartments under the severe authority of his teachers.

Whenever he had been bold enough to question one of Irene's decisions, she had replied drily:

"Staurachius thought it proper to act in this way. I am sincerely sorry that you do not agree. . . ."

Messengers scoured the empire, preceded by heralds in embroidered tunics, sounding their trumpets

Or else she replied:

"Staurachius decided on this, and I trust his judgment."

And she would quickly dismiss Constantine, after a few compliments on his looks or the elegance of his clothing, and with protestations of affection belied by the coldness of her hard eyes.

Who was this Staurachius, the emperor's rival? Irene had chosen him many years before as her adviser; she had loaded him with honours and titles, and this upstart whom everybody hated was the real master in the Sacred Palace.

Pushed too far, the young emperor tried to get rid of him, but Irene heard of the plan and her rage was terrible:

"This plot was directed against me," she shrieked furiously, "me, your mother! You were going to strike at Staurachius, but it was me you wanted to ruin, you ungrateful child, in your anxiety to rule! But I shall punish this crime with the utmost severity."

And she did as she had said. While Constantine's friends were arrested and exiled, the emperor was beaten with rods like a disobedient urchin and shut up in his apartments. Yet he was the rightful sovereign, and he was nearly twenty years old!

Irene felt certain of the future. She was mistaken. The army, indignant at the treatment inflicted on Constantine, demanded his release and recognition as the one true Basileus. So Irene, her heart filled with rage, was forced to abdicate, and to leave the Sacred Palace in haste.

But not for long. Constantine, who felt no hatred towards his mother, believed that she had finally understood, and he yielded to her entreaties. In less than a year he had allowed her to return and to live near him in the palace. How wrong he was!

During this time, what had become of the gentle Mary, the young empress? There was naturally no place for her on the throne and what the emperor did for her was, alas, very little.

Mary was unhappy. Constantine had little love for her, although she had given him two pretty daughters. She lived in dismal but splendid solitude; and among all the mosaics and silk carpets she longed for the old house in Paphlagonia and regretted the deceptive mirage of her brilliant marriage.

But her troubles had scarcely begun.

When the Empress Irene was restored to favour and returned to the Court she was accompanied by a charming maid-of-honour named Theodota. The girl was both beautiful and nobly born and in no time at all the Basileus was hopelessly in love with her. The wily Irene at once saw what she could gain from her son's passion. Like a spider patiently spinning the web in which incautious flies will be trapped, she wove a ghastly plot of which the victims were to be first Mary and then Constantine. Then the throne would once again be hers alone!

One day she went secretly to the emperor and asked to speak to him in private. She assumed an air of humility and had dressed herself in a simple unadorned tunic. After prostrating herself before Constantine, who had risen to greet her, she spoke to him in honeyed tones:

"It is no longer the empress who speaks to you, but your mother who loves and understands you. Alas! I am deeply distressed to have made you unhappy by forcing you to marry Mary. . . ."

As she spoke she kept a sharp eye on Constantine's face in order to discern his thoughts:

"I can see," she continued, "that your heart is now drawn by the lovely Theodota, who is perfect in every respect and whom I love as if she were my own child. Theodota is nobly born and worthy to be your empress."

Constantine bowed his head and listened glumly, without speaking.

"But," the hypocritical queen continued, "it would not be right for those laws which govern the life of the masses to be imposed equally strictly on those who sit upon the throne. Reasons of State may force a sovereign to repudiate his wife. The fact that Mary has not given you a son is much to be regretted. And perhaps public opinion would accept other, equally valid motives for putting her away. My son, I want to help to win your happiness, which is dearer to me than my own."

These words were well calculated to please Constantine. Seeing his mother's approval, he hesitated no longer—so easy is it for a man to accept complacently that which accords with his secret desires.

Soon afterwards the news spread through the city: "The Empress Mary has been repudiated and shut up for life in a distant convent." For, it was claimed, she had been guilty of an inexpiable crime—worthy, indeed, of death.

What crime had poor Mary committed? All the people of Constantinople vied with one another in their claims to superior knowledge:

"She tried to poison the Basileus," said one well-informed citizen.

"I can't believe that!" exclaimed another. "Everyone knows she has the greatest affection for her husband!"

"Yes, but her husband deserted her when he was attracted by the beautiful Theodota, Irene's lady-in-waiting. The empress wanted revenge. I have the information from a reliable source!"

"Personally I think her only crime was that she no longer pleased the emperor, and no one will change my ideas on the subject."

The official version, widely disseminated by the palace, was that of an attempted poisoning, discovered in time. But more than one citizen thought Mary was innocent and had left the Court as a victim of her husband's guilty passion.

Thus the grand-daughter of Philaretus, poor Mary of Amnia, disappeared. In her ephemeral sovereignty she, like so many others, had experienced the frailty of human greatness.

As for Irene, the first part of her plan was fulfilled. Now she had only to let events take their course: Constantine would slide down the path to ruin of his own accord, just as his mother wished.

* * *

The celebration of the second marriage of Constantine, the sixth of that name, disturbed Byzantium greatly.

Theodota replaced Mary on the throne and what Irene had foreseen soon came to pass. In the vast Byzantine empire, deeply bound as it was by Christian laws, this union gave rise to tremendous scandal.

"The emperor had no right to remarry, for Mary is still living," the people cried indignantly. "The ties of marriage are sacred."

"Constantine has two wives," thundered the monks. "He is openly living in sin and his crime is all the greater in proportion to his high rank! Woe to him through whom scandal is caused!"

And, since the influence of the monasteries was considerable in the empire, everyone soon forgot Constantime's undoubted qualities and saw in him only a prince guilty of indulging in a forbidden union.

Naturally, without appearing to do so, Irene was encouraging this agitation which was so useful to her plans.

When the emperor saw that he would not succeed in calming the revolt of the monks, his worst adversaries, he decided to use force: he had the most influential among them beaten, imprisoned or exiled. The people of Byzantium muttered, while Irene rejoiced to see hatred growing about her son.

It was on a beautiful July evening that the last act of the drama began: Constantine, worried and full of gloomy presentiments, came back from the hippodrome and entered the palace, followed by his escort.

Suddenly, a signal was given and the emperor saw the people of his own entourage advancing to seize him. But the young sovereign managed to escape and fled to the port. With a few faithful friends he embarked on a ship and gained the Asian shore. He was saved, but for how long?

Meanwhile, Irene, the instigator of the plot, had installed herself in the Sacred Palace and was waiting for her son Constantine to be brought to her, bound hand and foot. Then came the news:

"Disaster! He has escaped," she was told.

She fell into a violent rage and then she began to worry. What would be the reaction of the people, who still felt affection for their young emperor? Irene decided to risk everything; she threatened those who had taken part in the plot with denunciation to Constantine if he regained the throne. In a panic the men concerned took to their boats, landed on the Asian shore of the Bosphorus, seized the unfortunate emperor and brought him back to the Sacred Palace.

It would be pleasant to imagine a moving interview between mother and son: tender feelings in the one, wise advice accepted by the other. But the truth was very different!

In the purple bedchamber where he was imprisoned— the room where he and all the other imperial children had been born—Constantine was waiting. Then there appeared to him the last human being he would ever see: the executioner, in his red tunic, sent by Irene.

No, she did not desire her son's death. It was enough to remove him permanently from the throne, so that she might reign in his place. On Irene's orders the executioner merely put out Constantine's eyes.

The Bitter Hour of Disenchantment

So Irene reascended the throne as successor to her own son, after a most unnatural punishment. The old chronicler Theophanus recalls those days with horror:

"The sun," he writes, "was darkened for seventeen days and shone no more, so that ships went astray on the sea. Everyone said that it was because the emperor had been blinded that the sun denied the earth its light."

But the forgetful masses soon came to believe that Constantine had earned his tragic fate by his own fault.

"Our illustrious sovereign," Irene's supporters said, "has freed Byzantium from a prince who dishonoured us. Suppressing her maternal feelings, she sacrificed a guilty son to the greatness of the empire."

Thus interpreted, Irene's crime became a heroic gesture. An astonishing travesty of the truth!

The ambitious Irene had finally realised—and at what a cost—the dream of her life. She reigned alone over the empire. Let us take a look at her as the people of Constantinople saw her after the holy day of Easter 799.

After long devotions at the church of the Holy Apostles —before the sacred icons whose worship she had restored to the great satisfaction of the monks—Irene returned to the palace in a solemn procession and showed herself to the people in all her sovereign majesty.

She passed by on a golden chariot drawn by four white horses, led by four great noblemen. On her face, already marked by age, the skilful art of the cosmeticians hid the ravages of the years. Very upright under the heavy purple mantle, she glittered with gold and jewels and, in

the manner of the Roman consuls, she flung out hand-
fuls of silver over which the crowd fought even as they
shouted:

"Long live Irene, great Basileus and Sole Ruler of the
Romans!"

There could no longer be any doubt about it: she was
indeed *The Emperor*. But how heavily the mantle and the
crown would weigh on this lonely sovereign, this woman
grown old in the immense palace, where ambitious men
schemed endlessly in the shadows to bring about her
downfall!

*   *   *

That night, once again, she tried in vain to sleep. Oh
Lord, how long must she wait for dawn? The quiet
room, lighted only by the flickering flame of a little lamp
burning before the icon, was full of shadows. Faithful
guards kept watch behind the high bronze doors. In a
neighbouring room attentive servants waited. On the
trees in the nearby gardens nightingales were singing.

Why could Irene not sleep? Oh, the wonderful sleep
of former years and the awakening, fresh as the dawn
itself! Now she felt a little heavier each morning—a little
wearier than the day before, as if night had poured lead
into her frozen limbs. She saw again—why had she
noticed it?—the swift and graceful movement of Chloe,
her little servant, as she retied the loosened lace of her
sandal. Oh, youth! . . .

But enough of these unwelcome thoughts! Irene would
think only of her tremendous destiny, her joy in finally
occupying the supreme rank, her power and her glory.

But was this power, which she had so passionately desired, bringing her the happiness she had expected? She had to admit that it was not. Was this because it had been acquired by a horrible crime? Could the anguish she felt really be remorse? What traps lay in wait for the wakeful mind in that endless night!

"No," Irene justified herself, "God knows that I wanted only the good of the empire. My government is wise, my people love me. . . ."

The empire! At the other end of the world a Frankish king named Charles, whom they called the Great, had just been crowned Emperor of the West by the Pope. At the thought, Irene's imagination took fire:

"East and West. A marriage between the Empress of Byzantium and the King of the Franks would recreate an empire wider and more powerful than that of the Roman Caesars. What a wonderful union that would be!" But bitterness followed her exaltation:

"Shall I have time to bring my grandiose plans to fruition? Shall I have the strength? I am alone in this palace, surrounded by prowling shadows. My enemies long for my death. I see them tracing the effects of age, the ravages of time, on my face and person. What if . . .? No, I am not yet at their mercy. I would not be Irene if I did not defend to my last breath this crown I wear."

At last, the first signs of dawn appeared. The nightingales were silent. Irene called her servants. . . .

*   *   *

Barely two years had passed. It was now October 31st, 802. The night had started peacefully for the guards on watch before the gates of the Sacred Palace. Everything seemed calm. The city slept. In the palace the noise had died down. No light, no movement in the imperial apartments: Irene was staying in her favourite residence at Eleutherion.

Ten o'clock! A procession approached the gates. The guards recognised great officials, high dignitaries of the court, nobles of the palace and even some of the empress's relatives. At their head was Nicephorus, Minister of the Treasury. He presented to the officers of the guard an order signed, so he said, with the imperial seal. In it Irene declared that she had abdicated in favour of Nicephorus, who was more capable than she of crushing a plot which threatened the security of the State.

The officers were convinced, the gates of the Chalcé were opened and the plotters gained control of the Sacred Palace. It was the end. Irene had lost her throne.

Next day at St. Sophia, Nicephorus had himself hastily crowned by the patriarch, and the fallen empress was brought back to the palace as a prisoner. In the chill mists of an autumn morning the appalled crowd learned of the events of the night and demonstrated openly against the plotters. They regretted their revered sovereign, betrayed by the very men she had loaded with honours. Could Irene not take advantage of the rising to dismiss the usurper?

But she was too tired to fight again. Power had not been taken from her, she had abandoned it. To Nicephorus, when he addressed her in honeyed words, she expressed only a wish to keep her palace at Eleutherion.

"Of course," Nicephorus promised hypocritically.

"And, for as long as you live, you will be treated as befits an empress."

The new Basileus did not keep his word. He shut her up in a monastery. But so much did he fear her return that she still seemed too near even then; so he exiled her to Lesbos where she was closely guarded. But when Irene lost her ambition to rule she lost her reason for living. Less than a year later she died, a prisoner, deserted by everyone.

7

Greek Fire

FTER a fruitful cruise in the Aegean, lasting several months, the Muslim pirates of the island of Crete had returned in the Spring of 960 to their lair in Chandax. The fast, round-bottomed ships were lined up along the stone quays. The little town, its white houses crowded between the mountains and the sea, hummed with a thousand rumours.

The Emir Abd-el-Aziz first visited the mosque to thank Allah for his benefits, then gathered his men in the courtyard of the palace. There the booty was shared out according to the rules: first the slaves, then the gold vessels and precious silks, and finally the weapons. A great feast was held and, as night fell, the replete pirates shouted and sang under the twinkling stars.

At dawn one of the guards on the Tower of Omar

thought he caught a glimpse of sails on the horizon, but he hesitated to give the alarm. The whole town was fast asleep. The regular, reassuring waves broke in their leisurely way against the foot of the ramparts. A scented breeze brought the freshness of the mountains down to the coast. . . .

Meanwhile, out at sea, Nicephorus Phocas, strategus of the empire, was giving his directions to the Byzantine fleet, now passing wide of Chandax. The ships would return later, hugging the rocky shores of the island more closely in order to burst suddenly on the surprised pirates.

Nicephorus was a squat, swarthy little man, whose barbarous manners were the scandal of the Byzantine court. But he was a fine war leader, energetic and wily. The Basileus Romanus II, who trusted him, was wont to compare him to the crafty Ulysses.

At Chandax no one suspected anything. The sun was already high in the sky when panic-stricken fishermen reached the harbour and reported, to the general stupefaction, that they had seen a huge fleet in the offshore waters of the island. The emir, who was informed immediately, at first thought the whole story must be a hoax. Who would dare to venture into these Cretan waters, where his word was law?

But he had to believe the evidence when the chief of his guard, the faithful Ali, confirmed the danger. Blue-hulled ships with white and purple sails were bearing down on Chandax:

"There must be two thousand of them at least, and in perfect sailing order. It can only be the Byzantine fleet!"

Abd-el-Aziz appeared delighted with the impending danger.

"The good emperor has lost his head," he said, smiling. "Here he is, sending us his ships! We will take them from him. To regain them, he has only to pay a good price. By Allah, this is excellent news!"

But there was no time to be lost. The pirates, summoned in haste, ran to their ships. Sails were unfurled, oars dipped rhythmically into the waves and, as the green standard of the prophet ran up to the peak of the mainmast, every man took up his battle station. On the prow of the largest ship, whose bronze ram cut through the waves, the emir, scimitar in hand, led his men into battle.

As soon as he saw it, Abd-el-Aziz tried to outflank the enemy fleet by putting on speed. These were his favourite tactics. Soon the Byzantine ships, surrounded and hustled towards the coast, would have to manœuvre in a narrow bottleneck. They would collide with one another, causing considerable damage, and would fall an easy prey to the pirates.

It was very hot now and the oarsmen, bent double on their benches, their bodies gleaming with sweat, had difficulty in maintaining the rhythm set by the shouts of the leaders. But the emir could not contain his joy. The Byzantine fleet was compact, heavy and slow and he was going to surround it, thanks to the skill of his crews and a favourable wind. Soon the imperial ships, taken on the flank and pushed towards the coast, would be caught like fish in a net.

Yet the Byzantines did not seem to be worried. On the

leading vessel, at the foot of the mast from which floated the blue banner with a likeness of the Mother of God embroidered on it in gold thread, stood the imperturbable strategus Nicephorus Phocas. He lifted his hand and the trumpets began to sound from one ship to the next. Soldiers and sailors knelt, while the monks blessed them in the name of Christ. Then with one voice they chanted hymns to the glory of God.

"By Allah!" cried the emir, "they have reason to invoke the help of heaven, for unless their God performs a miracle they will lie this night in the prisons of Chandax!"

* * *

The hour of battle was approaching. The lightweight ships of the pirates, the caïques, wheeled about, almost within bowshot of the Byzantine vessels. One of them had drawn close to Nicephorus' ship. Suddenly a ball of fire whistled through the air and burst noisily among the horrified pirates. The emir took no notice, but Ali realised the danger. The caïque blazed up in an instant and the flames had a strange light.

"We must stop the battle," advised Ali, "and return to Chandax as quickly as possible. All is lost, they have the fire. . ."

The "sailor's" or "Greek" fire! The Arabs knew it well, from Tangier to Tripoli. They knew that it had been brought to Byzantium three centuries earlier by a Syrian Greek named Callinicus, and that the secret of this terrible weapon was jealously guarded. Whenever an enemy fleet had appeared in the Bosphorus it had been set alight and destroyed. With this fire the Greeks feared no one. Ali urged flight while there was still time.

But Abd-el-Aziz was not convinced. He had often captured Byzantine ships and none of them had carried Greek fire. In any case, the caïque might simply have been struck by one of those flaming brands used by all the Mediterranean fleets.

"We must flee," repeated Ali. "I recognise the fire. There is no shame in flight when it is the only means of salvation. The prophet himself fled from the Holy City, only to return to it later as a conqueror."

"The lion of the desert does not release his prey," replied Abd-el-Aziz, giving the signal for attack.

The Mussulman ships bore down on the Byzantine vessels. Nicephorus calmly allowed them to approach and then a long red flag, which flickered like a flame in the wind, was run up to the masthead.

The powerful battleships, the chelandia with their four banks of oars, which were the pride of the empire, faced the enemy in line abreast. Each had a gilded bronze lion's head on its prow, the jaws open, showing long flexible tubes called syphons. At the other end these tubes were immersed in cauldrons filled with a blackish mixture prepared in great secrecy in the arsenals of Byzantium.

Nicephorus himself had supervised the shipment of these dangerous receptacles; he had had them carefully stowed in the holds of his vessels and watched day and night.

"Light the fire!"

The lightweight ships of the pirates wheeled about

The hellish mixture of naphtha, bitumen and sulphur was lighted by touching the mouth of a tube with a bundle of flaming tow. At once a flame shot out like lightning. Men from the mountains of Pamphylia, dressed in asbestos overalls, and African Negroes, their bodies encased in leather, guided the syphons by means of iron chains.

The flaming liquid, leaving a trail of brilliant light behind it, whistled through the air. As it struck the target, it exploded noisily. The pirate vessels shuddered and flared up like torches.

All the Byzantine ships were throwing the fire, and from every side, for they had syphons on their prows, along their sides and in the rear, spurting plumes of flame.

Yet Nicephorus coolly demanded still more. He ordered the catapults to be prepared. Their missiles were glass spheres filled with naphtha, ballistae throwing out showers of sparks to revive the flames, and arrows which fell in a rain of fire. When an Arab ship, blinded by smoke, was suddenly rammed, Nicephorus' warriors rushed into the attack. Normans, Bulgars, Armenians, Tartars—rough soldiers in the service of the empire—plunged their lances into the boiling cauldrons. They advanced in a stink of sulphur, overthrowing the pirates and driving the crippled crews into the water.

Here and there the Mussulmans, accustomed as they were to hard fighting, refused to give ground. They threw sand on the fires and tried to quench the flames with iron plates. They formed a barrier of spears to face their assailants. But soon the fire had the better of them.

7

Hulls went up in flames, sheets and tackle tumbled, smoke enveloped everything. They were forced to abandon the living hell.

So the pirates jumped into the sea, but the sea itself was a brazier. A thin skin of bitumen covered it and the sea wind whipped up the liquid fire which surrounded the swimmers and set them alight, so that they screamed in agony.

Ali had been right. It was not an equal contest. The emir realised this at last when he saw a good number of his ships reduced to cinders and foundering in the waves. Filled with rage he hurried back to Chandax, to recover his strength in the shelter of its mighty walls.

*   *   *

Summer was coming to an end and Chandax was still under siege. The Byzantines had surrounded the town, destroyed the Muslim ships at anchor, repulsed all the pirates' efforts to break through the blockade. As the bad weather approached, the soldiers of the empire longed to return to Constantinople. But Nicephorus was adamant.

"We shall not return to our country," he stated, "until we have recaptured the island of Crete."

And, to cut short all argument, he had food and money distributed to his men. At the same time he sent word to the Emperor Romanus II, asking for reinforcements. He would not attack before the Spring.

In his distress Abd-el-Aziz had decided to ask help of the Muslim princes, and had sent Ali to plead his cause with them. One night, escaping the watchful Byzantines,

Ali had succeeded in leaving the island, but the days were over when the word of a caliph of Baghdad, Damascus or Cordova had been law from Spain to India. Ali was quickly made aware of this:

"My fleet is in a pitiful state," replied the Emir of Tripoli, "and I am unable to help your master."

"I am fighting the desert bedouin, who are holding my peasants to ransom," said the Emir of Alexandria, "and I must settle with them first."

"I have just ended a long war against the Byzantines," added the Emir of Sicily, Ahmed ben Hassan, "and I must have time to recover."

Ali, realising that he was wasting his time, went to Syria to seek out the Emir Saïf, the valiant warrior who had often defeated the armies of the empire. This was his last chance, for an offensive by Saïf might make the emperor recall Phocas.

Ali reached Aleppo and went to the palace. He explained his mission. But he was asked to wait. The emir had gathered about him a host of poets, philosophers and writers and was not to be disturbed for anything in the world.

Ali was left to wander moodily through the scented gardens of the palace, the flowery courtyards watered by clear fountains; and through the State rooms glittering with brilliant mosaics, their marble floors covered with shimmering carpets, and their furnishings consisting of furs, silks and gold-embroidered damasks. But Ali grew impatient. He thought of Chandax, of Crete, of his brothers engaged in a ruthless war.

At last Saïf agreed to see him. What! Could this old

man with the fat, flabby body and slow gestures, the downcast eyes—could this be the hero of Islam, nick-named the Sabre of the Empire? He spoke in a low voice. Yes, he knew Abd-el-Aziz and would like to help him. But, for the time being, he had signed a treaty with Byzantium. He must keep his word. Later, perhaps. . .

Ali knew that there was no hope left. He tried to re-turn to Chandax, but his ship was wrecked. The emir would never see his faithful messenger again.

The soft, scented wind which blows across Crete scattered the clouds and seemed to be driving winter away. Nicephorus was ready now. He had obtained the emperor's agreement to send him a hundred amphorae of Greek fire which had been stored in the Manganes arsenal. On the morning of March 7th, 961, after ad-dressing his men, he gave the signal for attack.

"I wish you," he said, "to enter a dead town."

So the fire was unleashed upon Chandax. Almost immediately the flat-roofed houses, the domes of the mosques, the spires of the minarets and the towers of the palace were all crumbling in flames. The inhabitants tried to take shelter in the caves, but the smoke stifled them and they rushed hither and thither under a rain of cinders. The fire flew everywhere, catching at clothing, hair and skin. Crazed with pain, some poor wretches plunged into the fountains, but the water, instead of soothing their burns, only made them burn the more. The darkness was so dense that fugitives wandering through the ruins found themselves back at their starting-point again. Exhausted women crumpled to the ground; dead children seemed to sleep.

And yet when the Byzantine soldiers scaled the walls and arrived on the battlements they found defenders in every tower, still ready to fight. A bloody battle continued for hours. In the morning, surrounded by the last of his warriors, the emir succumbed like a brave man, his weapon in his hand.

Crete had been reconquered. Byzantine garrisons occupied the town, while Greek and Armenian monks restored the faith of Christ to honour throughout the island. After a century and a half of Muslim domination the churches were reopened and the bells rang out again.

Nicephorus Phocas returned to Byzantium, where he was given a hero's welcome. He was acclaimed as a second Belisarius and, in honour of his victories, he was known as the Hammer of the Saracens from that day on. Who better than he to succeed to the throne of the empire after the death of Romanus II? Acclaimed by the people, crowned by the patriarch, he was raised to the supreme power.

8

An Unhappy Ambassador

 IUTPRAND, Bishop of Cremona, had been charged by the Emperor of the West, Otto the Great, with a difficult mission at the court of Byzantium.

His journey had been without incident and on June 4th, 968, his ship approached the Golden Gate. While the sailors busied themselves with their ropes and furled the sails, the bishop, who had stayed in the city before, never ceased to praise the beauty of its monuments, the splendour of its churches and the energy of its inhabitants. He was full of praise, too, for the eminence of the Basileus, Nicephorus Phocas, the terror of the infidels.

Liutprand was already imagining his imminent arrival and the wonderful welcome he would receive. The Golden Gate would be hung with silk brocade and the rich patrician houses of the Mesé, the grand avenue, would display their pomp. The imperial guards in white tunics, and the urban factions—the Greens and Blues—would form a guard of honour the length of the route, holding back the joyous crowd which would be shouting cries of welcome. The high dignitaries of the palace would come down to the quay itself to greet the new arrivals and escort them to the city.

But as his ship came into port Liutprand was aware of a feeling of disquiet. What was happening? No hangings on the Golden Gate, no crowd in the streets, no one on the quay. But here was a little troop advancing: a customs officer, followed by armed soldiers.

"Stand back, no one may pass!"

The bishop protested, gave his name and pointed out his status as an ambassador.

"We have had no orders on this matter," replied the officer brusquely, quite determined to prevent Liutprand and his men from passing through the Golden Gate.

After a little while, however, he agreed to send a soldier to the Sacred Palace to see what was to be done. During this time the rain had begun to come down in sheets. The bishop refused to return to his ship and stayed on the quay with his men. Hours passed. . . . The ambassador of the Holy Empire, soaked to the skin, could only show his indignation to a few indifferent or gaping soldiers.

At last an order arrived. The foreigners were permitted to enter the city. Liutprand leaped on his horse. At once the soldiers stopped him and forced him to dismount. Why? They did not know, but those were their orders.

"You are to go to the Marble Palace," added the

officer. "That is where you will live during your stay here."

Liutprand departed hastily, without even asking for a guide. He was soon in the filthy and tortuous lanes of a slum district, while the rain had redoubled in strength. He lost his way, asked for directions, and then wandered on until nightfall. At last, he reached the Marble Palace.

He could scarcely believe his eyes. It was an ancient and greatly dilapidated fortress. The accommodation at his disposal comprised a few miserable rooms with uneven floors and oozing walls, under crumbling ceilings which let in the rain. The furniture was poor and the service deplorable.

The exhausted bishop could scarcely touch the frugal meal prepared for him. He went to his room as quickly as possible; once there, he soon fell asleep, while the bats danced a sinister ballet round the mildewed beams above his bed.

On awakening the bishop sent for water. The steward, a Levantine with ingratiating manners, hastened to buy some from a water-carrier passing in the road. The price asked was truly exorbitant but Liutprand had no choice. What would he have said had he known that this unscrupulous servant was also a spy, who had to report the bishop's least movement to the imperial police?

Liutprand consoled himself in the thought of the importance of his mission. The emperor could not fail to receive him soon. But the days passed and the bishop realised that there is no diplomacy without patience.

*   *   *

At last, one day, the long-awaited audience was granted. Liutprand was informed that he must attend immediately at the Sacred Palace. He sent his people in search of a horse or litter while he put on his finest robes. But, incredible as it might seem, it was impossible to find a suitable mode of transport in the whole district. The bishop's secretary, a young Lombard priest, stated his views furiously:

"Do not go, monseigneur. The tempest is raging, it is raining in torrents, the streets are filled with mud. It is not becoming, either to your age or to your rank, to go to the palace on foot. These people are making a mock of us."

"I shall go, whatever the cost," replied the bishop simply. "Once must do one's duty."

And once again Liutprand walked through the wet and slippery lanes. He reached the gates of the palace. They were closed. The guards stood there, impervious to the rain, with crossed lances and joined shields. Argument, delay, impatience from the bishop, disdainful indifference from the officers, successive arrival of officious clerks, explanations, enquiries. . . . At last, Liutprand was allowed to enter.

The Basileus himself had no desire to receive this envoy from Otto, whom he referred to contemptuously as "the barbarian who calls himself emperor". He had given the task to his brother, Leo Phocas, Master of Ceremonies.

Leo had no wish to be pleasant. He began by laughing uproariously at the sight of the mud-spattered prelate, who seemed unaware of the incongruity of his dress.

Liutprand, controlling his wrath, excused himself and urged the importance of the message he brought. Leo became more conciliatory.

"Very well, the Basileus will receive you tomorrow. At this interview how do you propose to refer to your master?"

"Otto is my emperor," replied Liutprand innocently.

At these words the Byzantine jumped up:

"What do you say? You know very well that there is only one emperor in the world: the Basileus of the Sacred Palace. Your master is a chieftain, a prince, a king if you like; but can you compare one pale, flickering star to the sun of the universe?"

Liutprand did his best to defend himself. Otto had been consecrated, he had received the crown, sceptre and orb. But Leo would not listen. He departed in a fury, leaving the bishop crushed.

The next day was a holiday. The whole town was decorated with flowers in celebration of Whitsun. Liutprand thought of Christ's message: "I give you my peace." He tried to regard this as an encouraging omen for his mission, which up to then had cost him so many rebuffs.

So he went confidently to the palace. To his great surprise he was immediately conducted to the throne-room. The Basileus was sitting there, motionless. Liutprand prostrated himself. He was about to speak when a flood of insults rained down on him. Nicephorus Phocas had risen menacingly:

"Leave this place! Otto is nothing but a traitor, a scoundrel, a creature of the devil. He has taken my

Italian lands from me. But I swear to you that I shall exact vengeance. I shall crush him, do you hear, like an evil serpent. . . ."

At last, Liutprand found the courage to lift his eyes to Nicephorus' face. He saw a little man of swarthy complexion, with a nose like an eagle's beak and a stony gaze. He was shaking with rage. This was no time to oppose him.

Was the bishop to regard his mission as ended before he had even been able to explain his purpose? No, that very evening he was invited to a great dinner at the palace. He went there without expecting too much. At the end of the meal, the emperor, who had been drinking to excess, caught sight of Liutprand:

"You serve a very poor master," he shouted. "Otto is nothing but a faithless, lawless barbarian. And you dare to call yourselves Romans—you, the Franks, a stupid and savage people. . ."

It was too much. This time Liutprand raised his voice:

"Whether you wish it or no, it is the Franks who hold in their hands that city of Rome which gave its laws to the world. Otto is Emperor of Rome, as Charlemagne was."

Nicephorus turned pale at the outrage, the guests yelled their indignation, the guards seized the bishop and threw him out of the palace without ceremony. Liutprand returned to his gloomy dwelling in despair. The unexpected reception he had found in Constantinople plunged him into deep despair. He then resolved to send Leo Phocas a letter suing for help:

"Hear me once, or let me return to Italy, but for the love of God, let there be an end to this."

*   *   *

A few days later Liutprand was invited to the palace. Leo Phocas spoke kindly to him and asked him to explain the reasons for his embassy. The bishop felt he had reached his goal at last; he was eloquent and persuasive.

"Otto," he said, without giving his sovereign any title, "has recognised the greatness of Constantinople, the city in God's keeping. He therefore seeks to benefit the peace of the Christian world by marrying his son to a Byzantine princess. Thus, by the union of these two souls, the East and the West would live henceforth in brotherhood."

Liutprand stopped for a moment to observe the effect of his words. Leo Phocas and the high dignitaries who surrounded him remained silent. Then the bishop plucked up his courage:

"Naturally, such a marriage would presuppose certain conditions. It is the custom for the young bride to bring a dowry to the community—a dowry in proportion to the greatness of her estate."

Still Leo Phocas said nothing. Were the negotiations going well at last?

"My master," the bishop continued, "thinks that the princess should contribute to this union Apulia and Calabria, as well as Bari, Taranto and Otranto. Of course, Otto would retain full sovereignty over Capua, Benevento, Amalfi. . . ."

"What more?" interrupted Leo, who had been re-

straining himself and now unleashed his fury. "You
come here, you wretch, to ask the hand of a princess
born in the purple, for the son of a barbarian. And, not
content with that, you have the audacity to claim our
Italian provinces! Was such madness ever heard before?"

Liutprand protested and tried to explain:

"But Otto is a great king, the most powerful king in
the West. This union would be a pledge of peace. . . ."

No one would listen to him. He was conducted yet
again to his miserable lodging, where he was closely
watched by the imperial guards. As the weeks passed his
strength left him. He was sleeping badly, he had lost his
appetite and was suffering from the isolation in which he
was kept. He asked again and again to be allowed to
leave, but his requests met with no reply.

From the top of the tower with its broken battlements
he watched the sea, his eyes on the far horizon, dreaming
of an impossible escape.

*   *   *

But why was Nicephorus Phocas opposed to Liutprand's departure? It was not long before Liutprand
learned the reason. One morning he saw the fleet weighing anchor. It was carrying to Italy an army whose task
was to recapture the principalities taken from the empire
by Otto. The bishop concluded that his peace mission
was in vain and that he was now no more than a prisoner.

Not long afterwards, a messenger from the palace informed him that Nicephorus wished to see him—at Brya,

one of the fortresses on the Syrian frontier. Liutprand made his way there as fast as possible. As soon as he arrived he had to take part in the imperial hunt.

The region was mountainous, with dark forests and deep ravines. The sick prelate, weakened by the long journey he had just made, was forced to gallop full tilt. Nicephorus, vigorous and untiring, laughed at him. He was suddenly aware that the bishop was wearing a hood in the western fashion.

"Take off that ridiculous headgear at once," he demanded roughly.

Liutprand refused. Why should he obey? He protested:

"After all, we allow you to come among us with your long hair, your curled beards and your embroidered robes."

So now the two men were bandying ill-mannered remarks on the respective fashions of West and East. Nicephorus took the opportunity to rain down another storm of insults on Otto's head. But little by little his rage subsided:

"I consent," he said, "to your return to Italy."

Liutprand did not wait to hear him say it a second time. Filled with joy, he returned to Constantinople, only to learn that by the imperial order no ship was allowed to leave the port. What a disappointment! The bishop returned to his tower again, closely guarded. Moreover, the situation was growing worse. On the feast of the Assumption two of the legates of Pope John XIII had been imprisoned for calling Otto "Emperor of the Romans" and Nicephorus only "Emperor of the

Greeks". The bishop expected to be arrested at any moment.

One morning he was led to the palace. While he trembled in every limb he was greeted by Christophorus, a secretary of the imperial chancellery, who accused him of gravely offending the Basileus:

"Nicephorus Phocas," he said, "the elect of God, is the only man entitled to call himself Emperor of the Romans. You know quite well that at the time of the great Constantine all the true Romans left Rome for Byzantium."

Liutprand tried to soothe Christophorus:

"I assure you that if we have offended we have done so from ignorance, and not from ill will. But we have seen you putting aside the garments, the language and customs of the Romans and we thought you no longer desired the name. I shall speak to Otto about it and to the Pope and in future we will avoid any nomenclature which annoys you."

Christophorus seemed satisfied. Liutprand began to ask to be allowed to leave in good earnest for Italy. But the secretary interrupted:

"Shall we speak of this marriage plan?"

Liutprand could not believe his ears. Decidedly, these orientals were very strange: they flared up over nothing, they grew angry, they threatened, everything seemed lost and then, suddenly, at the moment when one least expected it, they offered the velvet glove and everything could begin all over again.

Liutprand renewed his efforts. The endless negotiations began again. At times it seemed that agreement might be reached; but then, at the last moment, Nicephorus made new claims. Finally, he was no longer content to reclaim Capua but spoke of Rome, Ravenna and Milan. At last, he dismissed the bishop without ceremony:

"Go and tell Otto that we shall range against him all the peoples of the earth, we shall destroy his power, we shall hunt him like a vicious beast until he flees back into his Saxon forests. . . ."

Liutprand left. He had finally been given permission to go, but by the land route, which meant a long and dangerous journey for him.

Even so, one last indignity was to be heaped upon him. The imperial customs officers ransacked his luggage. They suddenly came across some pieces of purple silk of fine quality.

"These materials may not leave the empire," said the customs officer harshly.

The bishop protested. He turned to Leo Phocas, who had been present when the Basileus had formally given him permission to buy anything he liked. But Leo merely smiled. The customs officers quickly confiscated the precious silks. One of them even added:

"These cloths are not made for barbarians."

The furious bishop could no longer restrain himself:

"This is shameful! Can a prelate of Holy Church be a barbarian? And, as for these stuffs, everyone knows that despite your prohibitions the merchants of Venice and Amalfi are able to procure them here without difficulty and sell them to us at a high price. Oh, they are not afraid of you!"

The sole retort of the customs men was to confiscate all the materials, not only the purple silk, but also those which had been gifts to the bishop.

Leo was careful not to intervene. But, when the time came to say farewell, he intensified his embraces and marks of warm affection:

"My friend, with all my heart I wish you a happy return to your own country. I hope you will always have a pleasant memory of your stay amongst us and that one day we shall have the pleasure of receiving you again."

Liutprand was so stupefied that he said nothing. He made haste to leave this city which he now cursed. A little later he observed without surprise that he had been given poor horses and that his guide was demanding an enormous sum to lead him across the arid plain of Thrace as far as the Greek port of Naupacta.

Crossing the rocky plains, the bishop had plenty of time to mull over his grievances. In the evening, at their stopping-places, he calmed his rage by composing a vengeful poem against Nicephorus Phocas, who had given him such a miserable reception:

"Oh, fool," he wrote, "black as a coal, ugly as a shaggy fawn, bearded, brutish, barbarous boor. May your arrogance throttle you!"

But Liutprand's troubles were not yet at an end: a long ride through wild country, a storm in the Gulf of Patras, an earthquake in Corfu, capture by Albanian brigands—all these awaited him. After six months of trials the battered Liutprand regained his pleasant town of Cremona in the heart of Lombardy.

Yet there was to be great joy for him in the future.

8

Barely three years after his return he learned that, following the assassination of Nicephorus Phocas, the new
emperor John Tzimisces had agreed to a marriage between Otto's son and a Byzantine princess, the beautiful
Theophano. The nuptials were celebrated with great
pomp and everyone cherished the hope—soon to be
blighted, alas!—of a lasting understanding between the
two empires.

For his part, Liutprand was entitled to believe that
his efforts had not been in vain, for peace and the
brotherhood of men are worth a lifetime of devotion.

9

Basil, the Bulgar-killer

ITTLE was left of the tsar's army when the battle neared its end. It had been fierce and bloody, but now the Emperor Basil was in no doubt that he would carry off a great victory. It had all begun on the morning of July 29th, 1014—that fine summer day when, after a hot pursuit, he had succeeded in surprising the Bulgarian army in the narrow valley of the limpid River Struma. The Byzantine cavalry had charged down upon the Bulgars and broken their ranks.

Tsar Samuel had put up a good defence. But as the sun went down and he saw that he had lost his finest warriors, the Boyars, wielders of the long lances, he fled into the mountains, abandoning his camp, weapons and booty to the victor.

Basil learned of the enemy's rout when he and the

horsemen of his guard charged the squadrons of Omurtag, the Bulgarian chieftain. Omurtag refused to lay
down his arms, but when there was no longer any doubt
that their tsar had fled, the Bulgarians surrendered.

Night was falling and the Byzantines had lighted great
fires on the battlefield. They sought the bodies of their
comrades by the light of the flames while monks lugu-
briously chanted the prayers for the dead. Once again
victory had been dearly bought.

The Emperor Basil could not be consoled for the loss
of so many good and brave warriors. He was trembling
with rage when his generals came to ask him if they were
to massacre the prisoners as was the custom in this
merciless war.

"Death would be too mild a punishment for them,"
replied the emperor. "Assemble them here, with their
hands tied behind their backs."

Basil returned to his tent and stripped off his armour,
his coat of mail and his tunic. Then, bare-chested, he
went down to the river, dived into the cold water and
splashed about ecstatically. Then he put on a pair of
peasant breeches and a goat-hair tunic.

Who would have known him for the Emperor of
Byzantium? Basil the Macedonian was certainly not a
king like other kings. Since his accession he had left the
Sacred Palace, bored by its strict ceremonial. He preferred the life of the camps and his reign was one long
succession of battles on all the frontiers of the empire,
from the plains of the Danube to the Syrian desert. For
more than thirty years now he had been fighting the
Bulgars and the stamina of this Slav race maddened him.

But now the fortune of arms had decided in favour of the empire.

"Let the prisoners be brought here!"

Basil's face was terrible as he gave the order. This stocky, sturdy little man, his weatherbeaten face fringed by a reddish beard, his eyes blue and hard, was accustomed to unhesitating obedience. The Bulgars, exhausted by fighting, were still stoical in adversity. When they had been assembled, the emperor pronounced sentence:

"Let their eyes be put out, so that they never see the light of day again. But let one in a hundred be spared."

The Bishop of Salonica tried to soothe the imperial wrath. There were 15,000 prisoners, who belonged to a Christian race. They had fought valiantly for their country and deserved to be treated honourably. But Basil would not relent. His orders were carried out.

Basil was feasting with his companions when the strategus Maleinus asked him:

"Why did you show mercy to one man in a hundred, Caesar?"

"That man," replied the emperor, stroking his curly beard with a familiar gesture, "will have to guide his companions to Preslav the Great, Tsar Samuel's capital. I can picture that strange army arriving at the palace. . . ."

And Basil, with a ringing laugh which shook his whole frame, invited his friends to drink to the approaching end of the Bulgar kingdom.

"It will not be long," said he, "before this nation of slaves is crawling at my feet."

*   *   *

But Basil was wrong if he thought that his cruel action would reduce a freedom-loving race to subjection. Samuel did not survive his defeat, but his son and then his nephew continued the battle for another four years. At the cost of furious fighting the Bulgarian towns fell one by one into the hands of the Byzantines.

But one day Ochrida, the last stronghold, was besieged and reduced by famine. The Tsarina Mary, who had been leading the resistance since the death of her husband, was forced to sue for peace. Basil agreed to receive her in his camp, among his soldiers.

She had been told not to expect any pity from the sovereign whom the Byzantines called "Bulgar-killer". She walked towards him, very erect in her mourning veil, followed by the royal children and the principal Boyars of the Court.

"My lord," she said, prostrating herself, "you have defeated a brave nation and we are in your power. But to be truly great one must conquer oneself. I implore you to show mercy, not to me, but to my people, in memory of Tsar Boris who converted us to Christianity, of Tsar Simeon who when he laid siege to Byzantium refused to attack the City of God, and of Tsar Samuel who was always an honourable and valiant adversary to you."

Basil appeared unmoved; but at the sight of this courageous woman, embracing his knees in the manner of the suppliants of old, yet retaining her dignity in her grief, he felt his desire for vengeance fading. He invited her to rise and assured her of his protection. He demanded that the Boyars swear allegiance to him, which they did at once.

"I wish the Bulgars to be our friends from now on," proclaimed Basil.

The emperor's merciful decision surprised his followers. He had finally realised that nothing lasting can be founded on hatred. And, above all, now that the war was over, he wanted to visit Greece.

Greece! There was not one Byzantine who laid claim to culture, learning, letters or art who had not been there many times, in search of the traces of ancient glory. The libraries and museums of Constantinople had collected quantities of Greek works. But Basil had never yet had the leisure to visit Greece.

He was not going there in order to enquire into the things of the spirit, however. As a child, despite his lively intelligence, his laziness had been the despair of his teachers. As a young man he had scorned his studies, for he thought only of swordplay and horsemanship. Finally, as emperor, he could speak Greek, but as a soldier spoke, for he had a horror of the pompous speeches usually composed by the Greek orators for imperial ceremonies.

Yet Greece attracted him, and it was there that he desired to celebrate his victory over the Bulgars.

"Greece," he said to Maleinus, "is the land of heroes."

So Basil first crossed Macedonia, that wild and verdant land which was the cradle of his dynasty. He recalled memories of Alexander who had set out from there to conquer the world. Then he saw Olympus, the mountain of the ancient gods, crowned with clouds, and he thought of the heroes of Homer—fiery Achilles and cautious Ulysses.

He journeyed on across the plains of Thessaly, passing

Thermopylae, the narrow pass where Leonidas, King of Sparta, had defended the freedom of the Greeks against the Persians. He spent some days at Delphi, at the foot of the shining rocks where Apollo's spring gushes forth. At Thebes he saw the house of Pindar, the poet of the Olympic Games; and the citadel of Epaminondas, head of the warriors of the long lances.

At last, one morning, he reached Athens. The sun was rising over the white marble Acropolis. Basil, at the head of his army in full marching order, set foot on the Sacred Way where the processions used to pass on the feasts of Athene, the helmeted goddess who was the watchful guardian of the city. At the entrance to the Acropolis the emperor was welcomed by the governor of the province (the strategus), the high dignitaries and the town magistrates (the archontes), who offered him bread and salt as symbols of hospitality. Then Basil went to the Parthenon, the great temple of Athene which had been turned into a Christian church.

"Welcome to the house of God!" said Archbishop Michael. "Glory to you, glorious Caesar!"

Basil entered the sanctuary under the cool gaze of the gods and marble heroes carved by Phidias. Where the great statue of Athene Parthenos had once stood, there was now an icon representing the Virgin holding the infant Jesus in her arms. The emperor prayed at length, thanking the Mother of God for giving him victory.

Then he sent for the presents he had brought for the Church—a golden dove, symbol of the Holy Spirit, which was hung above the altar, a golden lamp whose flame was never to be quenched, and a coffer encrusted with mother-of-pearl and ivory, containing holy relics. He also promised the archbishop that he would contribute to the repair of the Greek churches and the endowment of new monasteries. Meanwhile, the Varangians of the guard had remained in the forecourt of the temple. Wine had been brought to them and they were playing knucklebones peacefully on the sacred paving stones.

*   *   *

Constantinople was celebrating. Since dawn, the crowd had been thronging the great forum of the Augusteum near the Sacred Palace. The first arrivals had taken their places under the porticos, sheltered from the scorching sun; others, in order to get a better view, perched on the pedestals of the gilded bronze statues. The guards, clutching their lances, had difficulty in holding back the crowd which was pouring down the great avenue, the Mesé, to watch the triumph of the Emperor Basil.

At the order of the Master of Ceremonies, groups had been gathering for hours all round the forum: the imperial troops, the palace militia and the hippodrome factions—Greens and Blues—with their insignia.

Later the high dignitaries of the Court arrived, led by the chief minister, the Grand Logothetus; the patricians, senators, strategi, governors of foreign states, allies or vassals of the empire, all aroused a lively curiosity among the spectators.

"There is the ambassador of the Most Serene Republic of Venice, in the red surcoat embroidered with ermine."

"And the Lombard Prince of Capua, in the silver breastplate."

"There is the King of Armenia, in a white robe embroidered with legendary animals. With him are the princes of the Caucasus. See their fine faces and clear eyes."

"And there are all the Slavs, the Knez of Serbia, the Tsar of Croatia, and Vladimir Prince of Kiev, escorted by his Boyars in their fur cloaks. Praise be to God that the Bulgars have been defeated!"

Sacred hymns rang out, played on the palace organs. Choristers in their white vestments took their places before the chapel of Constantine. They were followed by the patriarch Polyeuctus, wearing an embroidered cope, and by bishops and priests and a long procession of black-robed monks, starred here and there by the silver of their crosses.

Suddenly, a great cry rose from the crowd. The emperor appeared, preceded by his guard. As usual, he was dressed as a soldier, but he had flung over his coat of mail a long purple cloak and exchanged his warrior's helmet for a narrow enamelled circlet. He sat down on a gilded throne at the foot of the column of Constantine, while all the onlookers cheered him with enthusiasm.

The cheering went on and on. When it died down Basil summoned the Grand Logothetus and ordered him to bring forward the prisoners. Everyone looked towards the praetorium, a vast building at the foot of the square, from which the Bulgars would file before the emperor in a long procession under the hot sun.

"Here they come! Here they come. . . ."

At their head was the Tsarina Mary, walking slowly, her sad eyes downcast. She was followed by the army commander, the rough Omurtag, and then by old Malamir. Next came the Boyars, laden with chains, and then men and women of the people, who had been captured in various parts of the country, often after fierce combat.

In contrast to their usual custom, the people in the crowd did not hurl insults at the captives: they seemed to respect the nation which had made them tremble for so long. Only when the trophies came on the scene did they give vent to shouts of joy. The imperial guard brought on wagonloads of bronze breastplates, great swords, battle axes and chased bronze shields. Grooms led the white horses of the Steppes, nervous and whinnying, and stable-boys held, on short leashes, Danube mastiffs and lithe greyhounds.

"The treasure, the treasure!"

A great carpet, glowing with colour, had been laid on the ground and an endless line of army officers piled upon it collars and bracelets of gold, coins, jewels, silks, furs, crystal vases and enamelled goblets. The Grand Logothetus, after having it blessed by the patriarch, put into the hands of the Emperor Basil the golden crown of Tsar Simeon, taken from the palace of Preslav the Great, the Bulgarian capital.

The moment had come for the choristers to intone the victory hymn, which the people took up:

"Hail, King of the Romans, whom the Holy Trinity has made victor for ever. Hail, incomparable warrior, glorious equal of the Holy Apostles."

The trumpets sounded, then silence fell. A strategus took Tsarina Mary by the shoulders and drew her towards the column of Constantine, forcing her to prostrate herself in the dust. The emperor, seated on his throne, looked down at Mary. As a sign of mastery he placed his red-slippered right foot on the sovereign's neck. But he lifted it again at once, and to the cheers of the crowd he gave her the kiss of peace.

All the other captives, at the orders of their guards, flung themselves to the ground and begged for mercy, while soldiers brought the conquered standards to the emperor.

"Who is great but our God?" sang the choir. "May God protect the Basileus, whose arms uphold the world. . . ."

The emperor declared his intention of treating the Bulgars as friends and respecting their customs. The day ended in a great ceremony at St. Sophia, under the golden dome where the candelabra blazed amid the fumes of myrrh and incense.

It was said that angels from heaven alighted on the altar that day, bringing to the emperor—the elect of God—their message of faith and love.

10

The Disappointments of Princess Anne

At the Convent of Our Lady of Grace

S my life draws towards its close and I leave the cares of the world further behind each day—now that I have said farewell to the Court and its deceptive brilliance —I like to withdraw as often as possible to the convent which my mother, the Empress Irene Ducas, founded and took under her protection.

There, among the prayers and pious meditations, I like to look back and remember my destiny, the life I lived on the steps of the throne and which some envious people regarded as brilliant and happy.

Now that I am an old woman I can tell you that my life was a succession of disillusionments and sorrows and that it began so high, only to bring me constantly lower. Born in the purple, crowned almost in the cradle, I saw the throne which was promised me at birth receding further and further from me; I suffered from the faithlessness of those whom I thought to be my friends and who deserted me in misfortune; I knew loneliness as death took away, one by one, those who had loved me.

*   *   *

I was born in Byzantium, in December, 1083, in the Sacred Palace. Naturally I first saw the light in the "purple chamber", as was the right of the imperial children, for I was the eldest daughter of the Basileus Alexius Comnenus.

The emperor longed passionately for an heir to the empire: my birth sent him mad with joy. From what they tell me, no princess has ever been so fêted. The palace gave huge presents to the senate and the army to mark the occasion; the people were loaded with delicacies and casks of wine and ale; and silver coins showered down upon the crowd.

Thenceforth, when their sovereigns appeared at the forum or the hippodrome, the Byzantines used to include in their cheers the name of the little Anne, the baby princess, who lay asleep in her cradle surmounted by the imperial crown.

How could I fail to regret the paradise of my early years? So much love surrounded me in my infancy!

First there was my father, the Emperor Alexius, whom I regarded as a demi-god—beautiful, majestic, clothed in gold, master of the world. I was overjoyed when he visited the *gynaeceum*, the women's quarters; never did little Electra regard the great Agamemnon with more dazzled tenderness. My father would tease me, play with me, give me some marvellous present, some bracelet too heavy for my little wrist, and then leave me, dazed with emotion and joy.

But as I look back I see above all the forms of women in their long silken dresses embroidered with gold, their soft hair dressed in coils or piled into heavy chignons. Scented hands caressed me, tender voices murmured songs to me and taught me my prayers.

There was my mother, the Empress Irene. She seemed cold and distant in public, for she did not like official ceremonies or receptions at Court. But with me she was gay and affectionate; even after the birth of my three brothers and my three sisters I was always her favourite.

Her close friend was Princess Mary of Alania, whom I loved almost as much as my mother. Was it not my parents' wish that she should be my future mother-in-law? The wife of the deposed Emperor Michael VII, she had a son, Constantine, to whom I had been betrothed at birth.

I loved Mary: she had beautiful blue eyes, a snow-white skin and such grace that in my own thoughts I compared her with the marble statues which adorned the palace and gardens.

Through my childish memories I see Constantine, my little fiancé. He was nine years older than I and he resembled his mother, having her charm and her splendid eyes. What a handsome sovereign he would have made and how proud I should have been to sit next to him on the imperial throne, as my father Alexius had planned on the very day when all the churches of Byzantium were thanking God for my birth!

Alas, I believe now that his beauty was more of heaven than of earth. Constantine, my gentle fiancé, died at the age of twenty, and I, who was only a little girl, felt deep despair. I had lost my protector, the tender companion of my games, my attentive guardian. But it seemed to me that I was losing at the same time the throne of Byzantium to which I had been born and which had been promised to me—the imperial purple which was my inheritance.

But no! Even if death had not taken Constantine from me I should not have become empress.

For in 1088 the Sacred Palace resounded once more to cries of joy and acclamations; once more the hymns in recognition of grace shown to mortals were sung in St. Sophia, and once again the people were loaded with presents and holidays were proclaimed. All this for a little, swarthy, grimacing baby, wailing in the purple chamber; my brother John, whose birth deprived me of the throne.

Of course, I was only five years old at that time and I did not realise at first that his birth was to be my downfall. My mother, the Empress Irene, petted me no less and Princess Mary cared for me as much as before.

But my father's appearances in the gynaeceum no longer gave me so much joy: pleasure was always mingled with bitterness as I saw him take the whining baby in his arms and kiss him or bounce him on his knee. He addressed

"Welcome to the house of God!"

to his son remarks which seemed ludicrous to me, speaking to him of the empire, the crown which awaited him, the throne he was to inherit. It seemed to me that when looking at me the Basileus had never worn that satisfied expression, that look of pride; my heart bled with jealousy. Gradually I began to suspect that this little boy, taking his first faltering steps across the embroidered carpets, clinging to his nurse's hand, was really to be Emperor of Byzantium one day.

A little later I knew for certain that my dreams were over. I was eight years old. I recall the ceremony in which my father officially dedicated John, my brother, to the empire. I see the thrones under their embroidered canopies, no longer the usual two thrones for my father and mother, but three. On the third, sitting very straight, his face looking pinched and small under the heavy crown, his frame tiny under the velvet of the imperial mantle, was my brother, the crown prince!

Duly lectured beforehand, no doubt, the little three-year-old sovereign behaved very well and graciously greeted the senate, the army and the people, while the crowd burst into enthusiastic cheers. Then he was led away. But I had understood. I wept bitterly at the thought that it was I, Anne, the first-born who should have sat thus at the Emperor Alexius' right hand.

It was then that I began to hate the little boy who had unknowingly taken what was mine. No, I would not willingly yield my place to him.

*   *   *

9

How bitter it is to look back when no hope is left. I was fifteen years old. The waves of the sea rolled and broke incessantly under the relentless light of the Bosphorus; so it is with our destiny, butterflies of a day as we are. How many changes had taken place since the day of my birth! The jealous earth now held for ever the mortal remains of my tender friend Constantine, who had left me so suddenly. I cried much, but then I became resigned; the study of literature and the teaching of the most renowned masters of Byzantium distracted me from my grief.

For almost a year I had been married to Nicephorus Bryennius, and I cherished that prince who had been given me as a husband for political reasons alone. Like me, he loved his studies. He had read widely and he himself was a successful writer. But apart from this he was handsome, dignified and easy in manner; he was a brave soldier and a persuasive speaker, worthy of admiration in every way. Since our two lives were to be united from then on, I was determined to help Nicephorus with all my power and to do my best to uphold our common destiny. If God chose to raise us to the pinnacle of power, I would respond to the call.

But between the throne and ourselves there was still my brother John. . . .

Many unjust things were reported about my reaction to the death of my father, the Emperor Alexius. God, who sees our hearts, knows what grief this loss caused me! From then on the world was dark for me. My sun set on the day when Alexius, the light of the world, was extinguished.

And yet there were some who claimed that, with the help of my mother and my young brother Andronicus, I tried to force my father in his death agony to recognise my husband, Nicephorus Bryennius, as his successor. They put it about that the dying man, when he refused, was roughly handled by us. They said that as soon as his last breath was drawn we deserted the mortal remains of the emperor. They said. . . . But what did they not say? Slanderers are always ready to spy on the great ones of this world and distort their actions!

What I can record is my mother's despair in that tragic moment. I heard her sobs at the death of a beloved husband; I saw her fling her imperial diadem on the ground, cut off her white hair and put on the vestments of mourning. I myself, when I relive that terrible hour in memory, seem to have been plunged into a horrible nightmare, and I wonder why I did not die at the same time as my dear father.

Why do they not also speak of what my brother John, the crown prince, did then? He was so impatient to rule that he left the dying emperor's bedside to have himself installed in the Great Palace. He had managed to make my father, in his death agony, give him—or did he seize it from his finger?—the imperial ring, and he was crowned in haste at St. Sophia.

They said he was afraid of us and had to make sure of the throne at once. But, if his claims were legitimate, what had he to fear?

My mother and I often spoke of my brother John and doubted if he could become a good emperor. He had certain qualities, but at the age of thirty he still seemed to us too frivolous, too free in his ways; sometimes his actions were quite embarrassing.

So this young scatterbrain would occupy the throne of Byzantium from now on, while I, the elder, whom everyone recognised as outstanding in intelligence and wisdom, was ousted!

My heart was filled with indignation and I made up my mind to recover the throne which had escaped me. Friends and loyal supporters joined me and we decided to get rid of the Emperor John. We thought we would be acting in the best interests of the State.

What a futile adventure that was, and how many blighted hopes attended it! The conspirators, after showing great zeal at first, soon gave way to fear. My husband himself began to doubt our rights and did not hide his hesitation:

"Nature has arranged things badly," I told him indignantly, "giving you, a man, the heart of a weak and timid woman!"

The emperor unmasked the plot and had its principal members arrested. Then he made himself appear magnanimous by showing clemency. As for me, my goods were confiscated, but they were quickly restored by the imperial grace—which was the worst of insults to me. My life was ruined from then on, yet I was only thirty-six years old!

*   *   *

I lived in a vacuum. Who is interested in a disgraced princess? Mourning followed mourning: first came the death of my mother, Irene; then that of my favourite brother Andronicus. Finally, I saw my beloved husband die, too. From then on I lived only among ghosts.

What can I say of those last years? I spent them between God and literature. Instead of the courtiers of former days, brilliant and flattering, I was surrounded by scientists, learned men and holy monks.

Here in the Convent of Our Lady of Grace, silence and peace hold sway and I find some consolation in the work I have undertaken: the *Alexiad* in which the figure of my illustrious father will live again for posterity.

Alexius was indeed an exceptional monarch and none will ever be his equal. He brought order and justice to the empire. He welcomed the Crusaders from the West as brothers. He drove out the infidel Turks. When he died he left a great void, a void which no one has filled.

Soon, no doubt, death will receive me, but my sad life will not have been in vain if I can finish this book, which will save from oblivion the names of an illustrious sovereign and an unfortunate princess.

*   *   *

History records the reign of John Comnenus (1118–1143) as one of the best eras of the Byzantine empire. Poor, jealous Princess Anne!

I I

The Remorse of Brother Tybalt

N the year 1204 a horseman of noble bearing, accompanied by a single squire, came to ask hospitality at the Abbey of Vézelay. The abbey lay in the shadow of the noble cathedral which was visited incessantly by pilgrims who came to revere the relics of Mary Magdalene. Some were on their way to the Holy Land; others were returning from Compostella with the shell of St. James at their waist, and with their faces tanned by the relentless sun of Spain.

The master dismounted and after a quick farewell to his companion he disappeared through the heavy gates of the abbey. Who was this distinguished visitor and what message did he bring? He was received at once by the prior who then spoke to him for many hours. Following this conversation, from which he emerged with his face ravaged and streaming with tears, the horseman put aside his scarlet mantle and silken surcoat and assumed the austere robe of the Benedictines.

Immediately afterwards, he took his vows. This man, who had abandoned a glorious name in order to become simple "Brother Tybalt", inspired the whole abbey with his piety and humility. He performed the most difficult tasks, and occupied the lowliest place; and the number of his prayers and mortifications far exceeded those required by the Rule. Brother Tybalt was generally regarded as a true saint.

At the beginning of the thirteenth century the only subject of discussion among the pilgrims concerned the great events taking place in Constantinople, at the other end of Europe. They spoke of the Crusaders, who had set out to fight the infidel and ended by attacking and ruthlessly pillaging the great Christian city. They spoke of Greece with its marble and its radiant light, where French lords had seized kingdoms for themselves and, in their enchantment, were forgetting their wives and their bleak manor houses.

It was the fourth time that soldiers wearing the emblem of Christ had sailed for the Holy Land, but they had failed in their mission. Their sin caused a great shame and great sorrow to Christendom—so said the pilgrims, for they were humble folk, shocked by the treachery of the barons.

And when such words reached the ears of Brother Tybalt his thin face seemed to grow still more haggard, his tall frame bent as if the weight of this iniquity was his alone to bear. What terrible secret lay in his heart?

What fault was he trying to expiate here, in prayer and penitence? He had told the prior everything in their conversation on that first day, and it had been an agonising confession.

*   *   *

How The Crusade Set Out

Brother Tybalt began his story thus: I took the Cross at the beginning of the year 1200. I was young and full of zeal. I burned to leave at once to fight the infidel and free the Holy Land. How long and dreary all the preparations seemed to me! Of course, I was well aware that there were many problems to be solved. First of all the ships: we needed a great many to transport the immense army of 33,000 Crusaders, with their arms and their horses!

But naturally we applied to Venice, since the Most Serene Republic possessed the finest fleet in the Mediterranean. Oh! Those wily Venetians! All they think about is profit. They pretended to take an interest in our project, assuming the air of true believers, but their conditions were harsh. 85,000 silver marks was the price they demanded to take us across the sea!

We accepted, in the hope of collecting this enormous sum, but very soon misunderstandings arose between us. Many Crusaders, distrusting Venice, preferred to sail under flags other than that of St. Mark. So it was that instead of 33,000, only 16,000 of us needed the services of the Venetians, yet we still had to pay the 85,000 marks, for they allowed us no reduction.

We waited on the island of Lido near Venice, racked by anxiety and hunger. We had to find another 34,000 marks before we could set sail. Would we ever leave? We were losing hope, when one morning we saw a golden galley gliding towards us across the green waters of the lagoon. It was the Doge of Venice, Henry Dandolo, an old man of dignified bearing, who landed on the island and spoke to us in some such words as these:

"My lords, promise to pay us—from the profits of your first conquest—what you still owe, and we will take you to the Holy Land."

Oh, joy! The Venetians were giving us credit, and we could leave! The doge's words were greeted with enthusiasm and we sang all night in the lighted camp.

The fleet was soon ready, with more than three hundred ships. But instead of taking us directly to our destination it lingered in the waters of the Adriatic.

"Why this delay?" we asked the Venetian captains.

They were at pains not to give us an answer. And we, for our part, did not know the arrangements made between the doge and the leaders of our crusade. The truth was that on our way we were to help Venice to retake Zara, a Dalmatian town which had rebelled. But we derived nothing, or almost nothing, from the loot of this city, for the Venetians had reserved the better part of the booty for themselves in advance.

Zara was a Christian town and we sacked it. Our leader, Boniface of Montferrat, allayed our scruples by explaining to us that it had to be done if we really wished to go on. . . .

But we had not yet left Zara when, on the first day of

the year of Our Lord 1203, messengers arrived from the Emperor of Germany. What did they want of us? They spoke to us of Constantinople and of a certain Prince Alexius, son of the Emperor Isaac Angelus, and the legitimate heir. His brother, we were told, had seized the empire from him by felony and treachery. But his sister, the Princess Irene, married to the Emperor of Germany, had pleaded his cause with her powerful husband. It was he who had asked the Crusaders to help him to re-establish order in Byzantium by driving out the usurper.

"Fight for Prince Alexius," they told us, "and you will not regret it."

But many of us protested:

"What have we to do with Byzantium? We set out in order to go to the Holy Land! Let the Emperor of Germany arrange his family affairs himself. Since he did not see fit to take the Cross as his father Frederick Barbarossa did, let him at least leave us in peace! We are men of Christ and not Byzantine mercenaries!"

I myself held the same views. I had taken the Cross to wrest the holy places of Syria and Egypt from the infidels, not to do battle under the walls of a Christian city.

But skilful arguments were put to us and I must admit that they made an impression:

"My lords barons," said those plausible speech-makers, "how can we confront the infidel if we have neither provisions nor resources? It would be better to obtain them beforehand. If we replace the legitimate heir on the throne of Byzantium we shall be doing an act of justice. Moreover, we have been formally promised for our pains 200,000 silver marks and enough provisions for a whole year. Thus, and thus alone, shall we have some chance of conquering Jerusalem."

True, this had to be considered. Even the most sacred cause cannot prevail without money. And then there was that sum we still owed to the Venetians. Moreover, this detour through Constantinople would not take much time; it would be simply a stopping-place before the great battle against Islam.

Some of us still questioned our consciences, however. Had not Pope Innocent III warned the Crusaders against the subtle wiles of the Venetians? It was the bishops of the army themselves who overcame these final scruples.

"Far from being a sin," they declared confidently, "the conquest of Byzantium is a work of piety, acceptable to God. We must not forget that an arrogant patriarch, Michael Cerularius, took it upon himself to reject the authority of the Sovereign Pontiff, and our brothers of the East separated from the Catholic community. Prince Alexius has promised to bring the Greek church back to the authority of Rome. Is not that a goal supremely worthy of the Crusader?"

The die was cast. Woe to him who refused to work for the union of the churches! Thus it was—and I shudder with shame—that the barons who had taken the Cross to fight the infidel prepared to conquer the Christian city of Constantinople, known as "the City in God's keeping".

*   *   *

How We Took the City

The morning sun shone down from a clear sky, sparkling on a thousand wavelets as our fleet sailed under the formidable walls of Constantinople. I can see that arrival again in memory.

On the quays, our unfurled banners fluttered in the wind, the drums sounded, the silver trumpets blared forth their battle-cry. It was a glorious spectacle!

As we approached we saw to our amazement that the townsfolk, far from fleeing in panic, were lining the ramparts, while all along the shore troops awaited us with an air of calm assurance.

What were we to do? Our commanders argued until an order came from the doge's galley, where the Venetian standard of the golden lion on its scarlet ground flew from the masthead:

"Forward, my lords! With the help of Almighty God we shall take the city!"

At once, armed soldiers leaped from the ships into the water, which came up to their waists. Visor down, sword in hand, they waded towards the shore.

When they saw the men-at-arms charging towards them, their brandished swords flashing in the sun and their pennants fluttering in the wind, the Greek soldiers immediately retreated into the town without daring to give battle!

Victory! Our army established itself on the bank, while from the ships the sailors launched wooden floats on which the horses were to cross. Soon afterwards we gained the usurper's former camp. No one was there!

All the Greeks had fled, abandoning their tents which were still filled with provisions. What merrymaking there was among our men!

"We have been hungry for so long," they said, laughing, "that we have forgotten the taste of a good meal!"

Next day we took the fortified town of Galata. This opened to us the entrance to the Golden Horn, and our ships were placed in safety. Now we had only to make the assault on the walls of Constantinople.

But we were no longer in such a hurry. Alas! We had forgotten the ardour which had caused us to don over our armour the white tunic with its crimson cross. Our men devoted themselves to a gay life, plundering, drinking and feasting amid laughter and song.

Nevertheless, we decided to attack in the middle of July. The Venetians told us that they held part of the city and we had only to come half way to meet them. It was too easy! Soon we saw a black cloud over the city. Then it turned red and burst into flame. A whole quarter of the city was devoured. The Venetians, attacked by the imperial troops, had been forced to withdraw, and to cover their retreat they had lighted a vast fire whose flames rose to the sky.

The Byzantines went over to the attack and there were so many of them that it seemed to us, as we watched them advancing, that they covered the whole countryside. We were in grave peril, but the enemy had not the courage to press his advantage; the Byzantines withdrew; it was a great miracle.

"Never has God saved anyone from such peril as that from which He saved our army today, and even the boldest of us must rejoice!" Geoffrey of Villehardouin, Marshal of Champagne, told me as we trotted towards our camp, exhausted by heat and emotion.

Soon afterwards the incredible news broke: the Emperor of Byzantium had taken flight!

"Thanks be to God," said the Crusaders. "The usurper has been driven out and we can re-establish the legitimate ruler on the throne. We shall receive the promised money and provisions from him and we shall resume the fight against the infidel, as we swore before God."

But it was not as simple as that. The young Basileus Alexius did not rule alone. He shared the power with his old father Isaac Angelus, who had no love for us. He was surrounded by people who advised him to forget the promises he had made to us. After all, was he not master from now on?

Summer passed, then autumn. The bad weather was beginning. What could we do without money or provisions? We had nothing. It was then that our men began to despoil the surrounding countryside and seize the wagontrains of provisions intended for the people of Byzantium. The pilgrims of Christ had become highway robbers, faithless and lawless!

Worse still! A few, in their cups, began to quarrel with the Byzantines and killed or maltreated poor people who had not been fortunate enough to find favour with the soldiers from the West. Indignation grew in Constantinople and one day a maddened crowd drove out the weak Alexius. A new emperor, determined to resist the demands of the Latins, put on the purple slippers. The doge tried to negotiate with him but he refused. Everything had to be begun all over again.

Would we have to attack the city—and at the beginning of Holy Week, too? Some thought this would be a foolhardy enterprise and that it would be better to reduce Constantinople by hunger. Others wondered if the Crusaders were living up to their name in laying siege to a rich Christian city.

Once again the bishops intervened:

"By taking the city you will be restoring the Greek church to the authority of Rome. That is a just war for Christian barons."

So on Monday, April 12th, towards mid-day, after praying and taking communion, we began to scale the ramparts. The Greeks took to their heels but, unable to believe in such an easy victory, we left the city after setting fire to some districts. That evening we saw the flames devouring houses, palaces and churches, while the poor frenzied people scrambled to escape the fire and the collapsing ruins.

We, the victors, returning to camp near our ships, stood watching the blazing city. It was ours at last.

*   *   *

. . . But Lost Our Souls

The rich Byzantines had left the city, abandoning all their property. All the palaces, all the fine houses belonged to us. Like the others, I now thought of nothing but the riches with which the city was said to be filled. There was a fortune under our hands.

"There are gold and silver table services," said one, "and precious stones amassed in this place as nowhere else in the world!"

"And the cloths," added another, "the wools and silks, the velvet and brocade, the mink and ermine furs."

"Not to speak of the pieces of gold," cried another. "The bezants, the ducats, the florins. . . ."

We were trembling with greed, but some grumbled:

"It may be that a lucky chance will take some to the richest houses, while others have to be content with meagre spoils!"

It was decided that the town should be plundered methodically. Everything would be scrupulously taken to three churches appointed for the purpose. Then the spoils would be divided in the fairest possible manner. So we went off to sack the conquered city. May God forgive us for what we did then, for we were as men gone mad!

*   *   *

Brother Tybalt was forced to stop at this point in his account. The prior respected his silence and his tears. Soon he began again:

I was with the group of Crusaders who were among the first to arrive at St. Sophia. Alas! Though the imperial palaces of Blachernai and Bucoleon were guarded by troops who barred access to the pillagers, the doors of the cathedral were open. Running in their eagerness, our troops dashed into the huge nave which was scented with wax and incense.

" There are gold and silver table services . . . and precious stones . . ."

Why did we fling ourselves on the holy images and trample them underfoot? We smashed the crucifixes and the statues of the Virgin on the marble floor. The relics of the holy martyrs were kept in gold and ivory shrines set with gems; laughing and joking crudely we flung the precious relics in the gutter and broke up the reliquaries, the better to divide them among ourselves. The chalices and censers and sacred vessels were filled with wine and we celebrated our victory with a parody of Holy Communion round the altar, burbling drunken songs.

It was then that one of us cried:

"Brothers, look at the altar!"

Then we saw that the marble was adorned with rubies and emeralds. Were we to leave these treasures to the Greeks who insulted our church? Certainly not. But the stones were so well set that we could not take them out.

"Let us break the altar and each take a fragment!"

And that is what we did. We led our mules and asses into the cathedral to be loaded with the sacred vessels, the costly materials and heavy blocks of marble. Certain beasts, too heavily burdened, slipped and fell on the marble floor. They were at once slaughtered where they lay and their blood sullied the church of Christ. Finally, we took the priestly ornaments—the mitres, chasubles and embroidered copes—and, putting them on, we embarked on a grotesque procession with crazy and sacrilegious dances. The division of the spoils was riotous. Most of the soldiers complained of the exorbitant claims of the Venetians and of the commanders of the crusade, who kept the greater part for themselves. And yet, as my friend Villehardouin said:

"Never was so much won from a single city!"

The churchmen themselves were no less fierce in their pursuit of relics. They thought they could attract profitable pilgrimages to their cathedrals and abbeys. I was sickened, I vow. I seemed to see the Romans at the foot of the Cross, quarrelling over Christ's garments. . . .

Indeed, Good Friday was approaching. On that day, in fact, the pillaging stopped. For the Crusaders, forgetful of their sins, Easter was a joyous feast. But I could not take part in the general rejoicing. I prayed God to show me a way of making reparation for my sins.

Soon afterwards Baldwin of Flanders, the emperor elect, offered me the Duchy of Athens. I was tempted to accept, for I would not have been sorry to become master of a city which has known such glory. But in my heart I knew well that honours and the responsibilities of power would not make me forget my remorse.

God is my witness that I took the Cross in no spirit of ambition or self-interest. That is why, after mature reflection, I have come here to Vézelay to be a monk as other monks in this abbey, solely concerned with my salvation. I beg you not to reject me from this community, where I hope to find peace!

"Have faith," replied the prior at last. "Your sins are great, I must own, but God's mercy is infinite. . . ."

12

Manuel II,
the Wandering Emperor

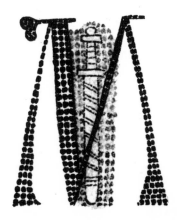

ANUEL II Palaeologus was a sovereign of fine presence; he was energetic, cultured and beloved by all—yet he knew that there was nothing enviable about his position. The Ottoman Turks were giving him a great deal of trouble. This Asian race, turbulent and fanatical, had launched into the conquest of Europe. In ten years they had brought Thrace, Serbia and Bulgaria under their heel and, in September, 1396, they crushed the army of the Crusaders from the West at Nicopolis. The day was not far off when Constantinople, beleaguered on every side, would itself have to withstand the assault of the infidels.

Already Sultan Bajazet, nicknamed "Lightning", had blocked all the roads leading to the city. He kept watch over the Bosphorus and waylaid the Italian ships which came to trade with Byzantium. So the activity of the port had been cut down, provisions and goods were in low supply, and craft and business languished. The people, without work or bread, were on the brink of revolt.

"What am I to do?" thought the discouraged emperor.

The treasury was empty. Taxes were not being collected, loans were difficult to arrange. In order to obtain a little money he had even been forced to pledge the crown jewels to the Venetian bankers. A solemn appeal for support had been sent to all the nations of Christendom, to help the empire to repulse the attacks of the Turks. But only the Grand Duke of Moscow had sent some money in response!

King Charles VI of France, however, wanted to show his sympathy for the Byzantine cause. He sent to Constantinople Marshal Boucicaut with a thousand men. This little band, which was certainly not capable of opposing the soldiers of Bajazet, was content to sack the Turkish towns on the Asian coast. When winter came the emperor had to tell Boucicaut that he could no longer either pay or maintain his troops.

Then the French commander put forward a daring plan.

"Why should you not go to Paris to ask the King of France for help in person?" he said. "Charles would not be deaf to your appeal, you may be sure; and he could give you a strong army which would enable you to crush the infidel once and for all."

"But how could I leave the city?"

Manuel explained that his departure would look like flight and would cause panic. He added that his nephew, Prince John, would quickly seize the opportunity to don the imperial crown and then to negotiate with the Turks. He also admitted that he had not enough money to undertake a long journey and keep up his position in the most sumptuous courts of Europe.

Boucicaut was at pains to allay the emperor's fears. He entrusted his best lieutenant, John of Chateaumorand, with the command of the French troops who would ensure the defence of Constantinople while Manuel was away. He succeeded in reconciling the emperor and his turbulent nephew; the latter swore to act as a loyal regent in Manuel's name. Finally, he helped the sovereign to collect by every possible means a sum sufficient to meet the expenses of the journey.

Boucicaut put in a great deal of hard work during the few weeks preceding the departure. He did it with a zeal which was all the greater because he himself was in a hurry to leave the East and return to the sweet land of France. As for the emperor, though reluctant at first, he was soon reconciled to the idea of pleading his cause eloquently before the Christian princes. Would this not be true to the tradition of the Palaeologi who, since their return to Constantinople in 1261, had always thought that salvation for the empire would come from the West?

*   *   *

On a fine winter's day in December, 1399, Manuel set sail aboard a Venetian galley. For reasons of economy he was accompanied by a small suite; but in order to disguise the poverty of his condition he took with him splendid presents for his hosts—gold vessels, silks and holy relics which he had not scrupled to take from the churches and monasteries of the city.

The journey was without incident, since the Turks had not paid any attention to the departure of the Italian ship.

Arriving in Venice, Manuel saw a town apparently floating on the water. The hazy light merely served to confirm this first impression. He saw the churches and palaces rising little by little from the lagoon and, beside St. Mark's Square, thousands of black boats with silver prows dancing on the waves.

From the towering pink campanile tipped with gilded bronze the bells called the nobles and people to greet the Byzantine emperor, the traditional ally of the Most Serene Republic. The doge, Antony Venier, in a purple doublet edged with ermine, his head covered by the golden bonnet in the form of a horn, greeted Manuel in the marble-paved square, between two columns, one supporting a statue of St. Theodore and the other surmounted by a representation of the lion of St. Mark. Then the doge presented to his guest the patricians of the all-powerful Council of Ten, the senators, the nobles registered in the Golden Book of the city. . . .

Manuel contemplated St. Mark's Cathedral, the work of Byzantine artists. He admired the elegance of the domes, the delicacy of the mosaics in the doorway, but he avoided looking at the four bronze horses which had once adorned the tribune of the hippodrome in the heart of Constantinople and which the Venetians had stolen in the sack of 1204. . . .

Then, with the doge, he boarded a ceremonial barge and sailed along the Grand Canal bordered with rich palaces. On the quays an immense crowd jostled in their eagerness to greet the Emperor of Byzantium. For eight days Manuel was received with feasting and kindness. He took part in sumptuous feasts followed by costume balls, and watched regattas in which the best oarsmen of the city competed in tournaments and naval jousts. He saw the sailors, fishermen and merchants of the port; he admired the work of the goldsmiths, the weavers, and the glassmakers of Murano; he talked to poets and artists.

But he did not forget his mission. As soon as an opportunity offered he reminded his hosts that he had come to ask for the support of Europe against the Turks. The doge, who had not given up hope of concluding a fruitful trade agreement with Bajazet, replied evasively. But he promised that his ambassador in Paris would speak favourably of the emperor's mission to the King of France. . . .

Manuel travelled on through Italy: to Padua, Florence, Genoa and Milan. He was received everywhere with open arms; but the Italian states, absorbed in the rivalries which divided them, refused to join in a fight against the Turks. Pope Boniface IX did launch an appeal to all Christians on behalf of Constantinople, but without result.

Would France offer more help? After a difficult

journey, Manuel, dressed all in white, entered Paris to the cheers of the crowd on June 3rd, 1400. He was housed in the Louvre palace and he discovered at once that his visit was most opportune. A treaty had just been signed with the English; the Duke of Orleans, the king's brother, and the Duke of Berry, one of his uncles, said they were ready to support the imperial mission. Among the French fighting men, greedy for glory and loot, the idea of a campaign in the East aroused great enthusiasm.

But what did King Charles VI think? A few days after his arrival, Manuel was received by the king. He found himself face to face with a young man who was about thirty years of age, and whose bearing was dignified and welcoming. The conversation turned amiably to Byzantium, Christianity and the Turkish peril.

But what was this? King Charles' eyes were strange; he began to tremble; he turned pale. He went on talking, but his remarks were broken and incoherent. Then suddenly he fell back in his seat, exhausted and indifferent, his eyes filled with infinite sadness. Manuel did not urge his case. He felt uneasy in the presence of this sick man.

Soon the emperor learned the whole truth. Eight years ago King Charles, as he rode through the forest of Le Mans, had had an attack of madness. He recovered slowly but had never been restored to full sanity. The Court festivities, and especially those which had just taken place for the marriage of the Duke of Berry's daughter, had exhausted the king and aggravated his malady. It was another of his uncles, Philip the Bold, Duke of Burgundy, who was the true master of the kingdom of France.

Manuel turned to the duke, but Philip would not hear of a war against the Turks. His son had fought at Nicopolis where he had received the nickname John the Fearless, and had been taken prisoner. To buy him back the Duke of Burgundy had had to pay an enormous ransom. Any venture in the East seemed to him doomed.

Nevertheless, he agreed to send Boucicaut a troop of twelve hundred men.

" That is all we can do," he said in a tone of finality.

*   *   *

Manuel was enjoying himself in Paris, but he realised that he was wasting his time. At the end of the summer, when Charles VI had another attack of madness, the Emperor of Byzantium decided to try his luck with another Christian prince, Henry IV, King of England. He made his way to Calais. Word reached him there that the English king would be pleased to receive him in London, once order had been restored in Scotland and Wales. But even at Calais everything was done to ensure that the Basileus would enjoy a pleasant stay.

So Manuel waited. . . . At the beginning of December he was invited to London. The city fêted him. The king took him to spend Christmas in his favourite castle. Henry IV bore no resemblance to Charles the Mad. He inspired confidence. He was a staunch knight, brave and elegant, who was as willing to talk of war as he was of poetry and music, which he loved above all things.

He declared his determination to support the emperor and he promised troops, ships and gold. But he took care not to name the date on which all this generous support would be available. He let it be understood that he must first consolidate his crown, pacify England and conquer the realm of France!

Manuel hid his disappointment and returned quietly to France. On the road to Paris he heard good news: Charles VI, apparently cured, was waiting for him at the Abbey of St. Denis. The two kings met again with pleasure and took part together in a great Mass before resuming the interrupted negotiations.

Manuel happily informed the patriarch of Constantinople of the success of his mission: "Our affairs are in good order, the troops ready, the commanders appointed; we shall not delay our return to the defence of our country."

But the days passed, and when autumn came Charles VI suffered a further attack. The project of a French expedition to Constantinople was abandoned. When the bells sounded for All Saints, Manuel, numbed with cold, returned to his gloomy apartments in the Louvre. He looked at the tapestry which hung in his chamber, portraying the gracious Goddess of Spring, her hair blowing free, her tunic scattered with roses, smiling in the midst of a group of little cupids, chubby-cheeked and mischievous. Spring! The time of renewal and hope. But was there any chance of salvation for the city abandoned by all, and yet so cruelly menaced?

Yes, when all seemed lost, hope was reborn. Christians who had escaped from the Turkish prisons arrived with the incredible news. Bajazet's army had been wiped out on the plain of Angora (the old name for Ankara) on

July 28th, 1402, and the sultan was now a prisoner. The victors were the Mongols, those formidable horsemen of the Asian steppes. At their head was the great Tamerlane, to whom Prince John, Manuel's nephew, had agreed to pay tribute if he would rid Byzantium of the Turkish threat.

There was no longer any reason for Manuel to linger in the West. He must return in all haste to his capital to rouse it to new life and prosperity and to foil the schemes of Prince John, who had proved himself an able ruler. He took leave of King Charles, who gave him gold, jewels and gems and promised him an annual pension of fourteen thousand crowns.

"Sweet land of France!" said Manuel, deeply moved. "I came to seek an ally and I found a brother. God save King Charles!"

After three years of absence, Manuel, the wandering emperor, returned to Constantinople. He now devoted all his efforts to opposing the activities of the Turks and to resisting them when they threatened the city again. And he succeeded, but not without difficulty. After a full life he ceded the imperial power to his son and entered the monastery of the Pantocrator where, under the name of Brother Matthew, he died in 1425. Never had such a huge and grief-stricken crowd assembled for the funeral of an emperor of Byzantium.

13

The City Threatened

IGHT breezes were carrying the fragrance of spring to the town when a few days after Easter in the year 1453 the Turkish army arrived before Constantinople and set up their tents facing the ramparts, from the Golden Horn to the Sea of Marmara.

From his palace of Blachernai, Emperor Constantine XI Dragases could see the Ottoman troops as they raced in by every road in a cloud of dust and then massed on the hillsides of Maltepe, on either side of the calm waters of the Lycus. Having left Adrianople, their European capital, less than a fortnight before, the Turks had reached Constantinople by forced marches, for their fiery young Sultan Mohammed II had sworn to take the city.

The emperor had at his side a high official, George Phrantzes, the Protovestiarius—Master of the Imperial

Wardrobe, a childhood friend of the sovereign and a skilled diplomatist. Phrantzes, who knew the Turks well, explained the enemy positions to Constantine.

"There, opposite the Gate of St. Romanus, is the sultan's tent, flying the red banner with its gold crescent. There are the janissaries, their finest soldiers, skilled in the use of the lance, the dagger and the curved sword, or yataghan. . . ."

Then Phrantzes enumerated the other troops who covered the field: the Turkish and Afghan horsemen, the rough mountain people of Anatolia, the Thracian archers and the crowd of bashi-bazouks—mercenaries and adventurers from every land who had entered the service of the sultan in the hope of rich spoils. He spoke of the commanders whose standards he could see: the old Vizier Halil, the ambitious Zagan, the cruel Kharadja.

"There is no doubt about it," he said, "the whole Turkish army is there."

"Yes, it was bound to happen one day."

The emperor now realised that a decisive battle had begun. Mohammed II had made no secret of his determination to take the city; to succeed where his predecessors—even Bajazet and Murad—had failed. He would complete the Ottoman victory. The Turks had already wrested from Constantinople all the land surrounding it and had reduced it to a mere Christian enclave in a Muslim land. They had the town at their mercy.

A few months before, Mohammed had defined his intentions. His grandfather had built one fortress on the

Asian shore of the Bosphorus and he himself had another built on the European shore, thus cutting off the town from all trade with the West. Constantine protested, but he still remembered with humiliation the young sultan's retort:

"What right have you to meddle with such things? Both shores are mine: the Asian because it is inhabited by my people, the European because you are unable to defend it."

"The city will be defended, at all events," murmured the emperor; "fight as he may, the Turk shall not take it."

Constantine knew that everything possible had been done to reinforce the defences. The great wall, which had been derelict in places, had been repaired. With its double ramparts, its wide moat and its ninety-six towers, it had already repulsed many attackers over ten centuries. There was nothing to fear from the sea, for an iron chain, stretched between the towers of Mangana and Galata, barred the Golden Horn to the Turkish ships.

But what activity there was in the enemy camp! The tents had been pitched, the fires lighted and a trench dug between the camp and the town to avoid any possibility of surprise. And now countless wagons were arriving, drawn by horses and buffaloes, bringing provisions, weapons and engines of war: all the equipment for a siege. Phrantzes tried to reassure the emperor.

"The Turks have cannon, it is true, but they cause more fright than damage."

"Nevertheless," Constantine remarked, "they are

boasting that they will reduce our walls to dust with the help of an enormous engine which they call 'the Royal'."

"Yes, that is the cannon which defeated Orban the Hungarian. They say that it can hurl a stone ball weighing twelve hundred pounds over a distance of more than a league. But it is fired only once in three hours and, in that time, we shall easily be able to repair the breaches in our walls. In any case, we shall bombard the enemy with Greek fire from our catapults."

There was silence in the Turkish camp after the call of the muezzins: it was the hour of prayer. One hundred and fifty thousand men fell on their knees and prayed, facing towards Mecca. From the ramparts the Byzantines watched the extraordinary spectacle.

"No, it is not possible," stated the emperor. "The infidel will not take the God-guarded city. Christendom will not permit it!"

But in his heart of hearts Constantine was troubled. In order to win the support of the West he had, in 1452, consented to the Union of the Churches. And many Greeks blamed him for this. In any case, could he really count on the Latins? Had they not shown their contempt for the Byzantines since the ill-fated crusade of 1204? Constantine well knew that he could not expect much help from Pope Nicholas V or from Henry IV of England, or Charles VII of France.

"Venice will support us," asserted Phrantzes, trying to give the king confidence. "The doge Foscari has promised to send us ten galleys soon, under the command of his best admiral."

"But is that definite? Not everyone thinks so."

"The Venetians will not move if they think it is in their interest to reach agreement with the Turks."

The man who had just stated his viewpoint so vehemently was the emperor's brother-in-law, Grand Duke Notaras. He commanded the Byzantine fleet, now reduced to a dozen ill-equipped ships, and he favoured a compromise with the Turks. He had no love for the Latins. He had even been heard to declare:

"Better the turban of Mohammed than the Papal tiara!"

But he realised that the young sultan, greedy for glory, would not agree to raise the siege unless he was forced to do so. The duke had therefore conceived an idea which he outlined to the emperor:

"One of my men saw the Grand Vizier Halil Pasha on my behalf yesterday. He has always had some sympathy with us. He distrusts the ambition of the young sultan who, in any case, prefers the second vizier, the brutal Zagan. Halil is prepared, if you wish it, to persuade Mohammed to raise the siege of the city."

"And what am I to do in exchange?" asked Constantine, intrigued by the suggestion.

"Little enough. Under the pretext of showing the Turks that we have plenty of provisions you will send fine fish to Halil—taking care to stuff them with gold pieces. The Vizier will eat the fish and put the gold in his coffers!"

"And what will he do for us?"

"Halil is old and considered to be wise. He will say that a powerful Hungarian army is coming to the aid of

Constantinople; that we have some terrifying weapons which will ensure our victory, and that the sultan, ambitious youth that he is, is preparing to let the best troops of the Ottoman empire be massacred."

"What will happen then?"

"The janissaries, as a sign of revolt, will overturn the cauldron round which they gather. They will demand to return to Adrianople and Mohammed will have to give up this conquest which means so much to him."

Phrantzes did not agree, and said so. The stratagem conceived by Notaras did not seem to him to be workable.

"Halil will take our money and do nothing," he said. "The janissaries are not afraid of death, for it guarantees them entry into the paradise of the heroes of a holy war. No, we must count only on ourselves and on our friends in the West."

The emperor thanked the two men for their advice. He praised their frankness, but refused to side more with one than the other. He asked Phrantzes to send an urgent appeal to the Venetians and gave Notaras a bag of gold to win the support of the Vizier Halil. He had a proclamation read throughout Constantinople, announcing that every man should consider himself mobilised for the defence of the city:

"One Constantine founded the city," he said. "Another Constantine will save it."

14

The City Besieged

NDER the impact of a massive stone cannon-ball, part of the battlements crumbled, leaving a breach in the ramparts. The Byzantine defenders rushed to repair the damage, pouring earth, pebbles and wood into the gap. The Turks had made a wooden siege tower facing the walls, from which the archers and arquebusiers were shooting at the men on the ramparts.

"Curses on the infidel!" shouted a Greek soldier.

The siege had lasted fifty-two days and on the Byzantine side there was great weariness. The citizens who had been commandeered to mount guard on the ramparts no longer hid their discontent. They knew that their families down in the town were in need, and they took the least opportunity to abandon their posts, feigning illness or poverty so great that it made it impossible for them to spend time up there on the walls without work or money. Their commanders spoke of the interests of the people, but they replied:

"What does Christianity mean to us, when our families are dying of hunger!"

Yet despite this attitude the city was holding out well. The Turkish cannon were numerous but their aim was poor. As for the great piece called "the Royal", it had exploded after a few days, killing its inventor. The sultan, who expected great things of his artillery, was disappointed and the Grand Vizier Halil Pasha, won over to the Court of Byzantium by gold, advised him to raise the siege. But Mohammed was adamant:

"I cannot withdraw," he said. "I shall take the city, or it will take me, dead or alive!"

Mohammed decided to launch his troops into the assault on Constantinople, but this time he was determined that victory should reward his efforts. He remembered that a few weeks earlier he had met defeat, thanks to inadequate preparation. Great numbers of his janissaries had fallen by the ramparts, and the Turkish ships had been broken against the chain which barred the Golden Horn.

This was the reason for the great activity in the Turkish camp. While the janissaries exercised in good order near the Gate of St. Romanus which the cannonballs had damaged, the bashi-bazouks were assembling not far from the ramparts the equipment necessary for the attack: branches to be laid across the ditches, ladders, rope, grappling irons for the walls, and mobile wooden towers from which to rain down arrows on the defenders.

The sun's rays filtered through great black clouds. In his red tent, its floor covered with sumptuous carpets, the sultan, who had been riding all day among his troops to encourage them, had decided to take a brief rest. Mohammed II closed his eyes as he sipped his mint tea. Commander of the powerful Ottoman army and leader of the believers of Islam at the age of twenty-one, the sultan was well aware of the heavy burden which lay on his shoulders; yet, in his heart of hearts, he felt a kind of secret intoxication as a result of the glory of his position.

Mohammed was indeed aware of his strength. He was young, energetic and able. His face, dark beneath the white turban, revealed a finely-tempered spirit: broad brow, nose like an eagle's beak, eyebrows arched over deep-set eyes, ruddy moustache and strong-willed chin. Yet the trembling hands betrayed anxiety. Had all the necessary preparations been made? Was the Turkish army really about to capture the Christian city which had so often repulsed its assailants?

"Are our ships ready for combat?"

Mohammed put the question to Grand Admiral Chamouza, whom he had summoned to receive his final orders.

"When you give the order," replied Chamouza, "our vessels will advance to the attack, some from the Bosphorus, others from the Golden Horn, since—with the help of Allah—we have succeeded in surprising the enemy from that side."

Mohammed II smiled. He thought of the night when he had organised the passage of more than seventy ships overland, past the hill of Pera to the Golden Horn. By means of ropes and stays the Turkish galleys had been hauled along wooden slipways greased with tallow. The Genoese, occupying the suburb of Galata, watched the operation but prudently did not interfere. As for the Byzantines, they suspected nothing.

"It was a strange sight," said the sultan, "and I shall not soon forget it. Our ships appeared to be sailing across the fields. When they had passed the hill and reached the Golden Horn at last, our sailors burst into joyous song because they knew that the enemy was at our mercy."

The sultan explained to Chamouza what he expected of him. While the body of the Turkish fleet would guard the Bosphorus to repel any Venetian galleys which attempted action, the vessels which had reached the Golden Horn would sail under the walls of the town to force the defenders to disperse along the full length of the sea front. Then the assault would be made on the landward ramparts and the war-cry: "Allah Akbar! God is Great!" would ring out.

Yet, before invading the city with his troops, the sultan gathered the members of his Council in his tent. The Grand Vizier Halil Pasha, looking downcast and disillusioned, put forward his viewpoint once again: the capture of Constantinople would be a mistake, for it would unite the Latins in a common hatred of the Turks, who would swiftly lose all their conquests in Europe.

"I beg you, for the last time," he said to the sultan: "raise the siege before misfortune descends on us!"

At once the second vizier, Zagan Pasha, intervened fiercely. He said he was speaking in the name of the young army commanders, who were opposed to any compromise with Constantinople:

"Why be alarmed, my lord? Allah is with you! Do you not see the strength and numbers of your army? The Latins will not interfere. Do not lose heart: we shall conquer!"

The officers of the janissaries confirmed that their troops were burning with desire to join battle as quickly as possible and they begged the sultan to allow the victors to loot the city. So it was decided: the attack would begin soon after midnight. The janissaries, after taking the city, would have three days in which to sack it and amass huge spoils. Then they were to return to the rough discipline and austere life of the camps. While they waited for the moment of attack the men would feast; then, soon after midnight, they would take a short necessary rest. From now on the cannon would cease to fire their shot.

"Let deepest silence prevail throughout the camp," ordered Mohammed, "and let every man sleep or pray."

With only a few hours to wait for the decisive battle, Zagan was very happy, for he was confident of victory. Halil was disappointed and sent warning to his Byzantine friends that they must expect a sudden attack. Mohammed II was nervous and troubled, so much so that one of his dervishes, expert in the art of calming

his master in distress, took the sultan in his arms, laid
him on his couch and rocked him like a baby.

15

The City Assailed

ISTENING glumly to the flattery of his courtiers, the emperor Constantine XI was nevertheless well aware that the moment of attack was near. This cheerless spring day—it was now May 28th—had given him no great reason for hope. After a night when his sleep had been troubled by strange nightmares, he woke to find himself, not in Blachernai Palace, which was too near the ramparts and exposed to the Turkish cannon-balls, but in the Sacred Palace in the very heart of the city. Constantine disliked this huge building with its dilapidated salons and overgrown gardens. He felt ill at ease in the consistory, where Justinian had once dazzled his guests with the majesty of their surroundings: the tiles and mosaics had fallen to pieces long since and spiders spun their webs on the gold and azure ceiling.

Nevertheless, on awakening, the emperor had found

all the high dignitaries assembled at the door of his apartments in the order prescribed by the Master of Ceremonies. The Turks were at the gates but the life of the Court continued inexorably with all its rites.

So Constantine crossed the town and there, too, nothing seemed to have changed. The Mesé, the great street of business, was still very lively: the women elegant, the passers-by careless. But here came a few dozen Greek soldiers, emerging from the church of the Holy Apostles where they were billeted and marching off down the street with a martial air. Their leader, Demetrios Kantacuzenus, a great lord with a haughty air, wore a gold breastplate and rode a richly caparisoned charger. The crowd cheered. How could they fail to feel safe when they had such splendid-looking troops to protect them?

The emperor himself did not share their confidence. What effective force could he send against the huge Turkish army? His troops consisted of some nine thousand men, of whom barely half were Greeks. Indeed, the most valiant were the Venetians, the Catalans and above all the seven hundred Genoese mercenaries at the Gate of St. Romanus, under the command of John Giustiniani. Truly, God's help would be needed if they were to save the city.

That is why Constantine had asked the heads of the Byzantine church for help. They came to the palace soon after mid-day. The Turks? Who was worrying about them? First the churchmen protested against the union with Rome and demanded that the emperor should dismiss the papal legate, Cardinal Isidore. Then in the course of the conversation they began to argue among themselves about certain verbal subtleties. The monks were the most overwrought and would soon have come to insults and blows had the patriarchs not recalled them to greater dignity. The emperor, with some difficulty, at last obtained satisfaction: public prayers would be offered immediately in all the churches of the city.

As night was falling, news came from the ramparts that the Turks were preparing for the attack. A great procession filed passed the forum. A statue of the Virgin, carried on men's backs, headed the long cavalcade. The crowd sang and prayed, raising their eyes to Heaven, where great black clouds were sailing past. Suddenly the storm broke; lightning flashed, and the statue slipped and fell to the ground. It was raised again with great difficulty as the rain redoubled its strength; it fell again as the onlookers watched, dumb with horror. Was not this the most baleful of omens? But the storm passed. The bells rang out in a full peal. A huge crowd gathered before the church of St. Sophia: senators, merchants, monks, Greek and foreign soldiers, great lords and men of the people.

"May God protect us," they murmured, "from the assault of the infidels!"

His voice shaking with emotion, the Emperor Constantine addressed them all:

"I exhort you to resist the evil Turks with courage. You must help to save our beloved city, Queen of Cities. Remember that the courage of the Greek nation once put to flight the countless legions of the Persians."

Then the Basileus turned to the Italian soldiers, drawn up in good order before him:

"Illustrious brothers whom we cherish in God, valiant soldiers of the faith, I call upon you to help us!"

The soldiers vowed to fight to the death. On a sudden impulse Greeks and Latins, united in brotherly emotion, fell into one another's arms. They entered the brightly lighted church, where they prayed and took Communion. Then they returned to the ramparts.

Midnight. The rain was falling heavily now. The Turkish camp was growing lively again. Torches were lighted, shouts rang out, armed troops rallied to the sound of trumpets and pipes. The cannons reopened fire on the city.

The bashi-bazouks received the order to attack first. They charged, yelling, along the whole front of the landward wall. They attacked in their thousands, but the moat stopped them. They tried to cross it with ladders while the defenders showered down on them a hail of arrows, crossbow shafts and lead shot.

The bashi-bazouks kept on coming, and their corpses began to pile up in the moat. The Greeks reduced the pile of bodies with hooks and pitchforks, but in some places the Turks succeeded in reaching the foot of the encircling wall, over the bodies of their dead. When they tried to scale it they were repulsed everywhere. By half past one the first assault had been broken.

Giustiniani was the organiser of the defence. He had concentrated the strength of his forces in the centre, where he expected the attack, between the Charisian Gate and the Gate of St. Romanus. He had arranged his troops in the *peribolus*, the space between the two lines of ramparts which protected the city. As a wise precaution he closed the gates on the town side. No one could escape; they would all have to fight.

During the first engagement the emperor had ordered all the bells of the city to sound the alarm, but the Byzantines had so often been roused for nothing that they took no notice. No one thought of joining the combatants. Everyone went peacefully back to sleep. . . .

Three o'clock. The battle began again. Now it was the Anatolian troops who attacked; to cover their advance, cannon-balls and arrows were fired against the ramparts. Through the breaches thus made the Turkish soldiers reached the peribolus, roaring their victory cry: "*Allah! Ilallah!*"

But Giustiniani's Genoese and Kantacuzenus' Greeks held them and then repulsed them. To the north, near the Golden Horn, the Vizier Zagan had attacked Blachernai Palace. He had suffered a devastating repulse and Halil Pasha was delighted.

Four o'clock. Dawn was breaking. Mohammed himself led the last and finest of his troops into battle. So the janissaries advanced with rhythmic step. Each wore a linen tunic, belted at the waist, baggy trousers, and a white felt bonnet curiously adorned with a wooden spoon, bearing witness that the sultan was their provider. Their commanders were recognisable by the feathers they wore in their bonnets. Their weapons were as varied as their own peculiar gifts: they included the bow, the lance, the musket, the yataghan and the dagger.

When they were within bowshot of the ramparts they loosed their arrows. The sky was darkened by countless missiles. Then the last attack was launched. The defenders stood their ground well, but little by little they began to yield at the Gate of Charisius. Giustiniani appealed for help. Reinforcements arrived, but in the press of battle they had left one gate, the Circus Gate, unguarded. The Turks did not let such an opportunity pass. They entered the peribolus in their thousands, taking the defenders in the rear.

The emperor was at the Gate of St. Romanus, where the Turks were repulsed with heavy losses. Giustiniani fell at his side, struck in the chest by a bullet. The Genoese, whose lifeblood was flowing away fast, decided to have his wound dressed in the town. Constantine begged him to remain at his post, but he refused. The defenders, having lost their leader, were seized with panic. They thought only of flight.

"*Kyrie eleison!*" they cried frantically. "The city is lost!"

The Turks methodically occupied the ramparts, slaughtering the Latin and Greek contingents who were still resisting. Mohammed's standard was already flying above the palace of Blachernai.

Constantine, rallying Kantacuzenus' troops with great difficulty, saw the Turks pouring in from all sides.

"What?" he said. "The city taken—and I still live?"

He tore off his imperial robes, with the exception of his red ankle boots. Sword in hand, he rushed upon the janissaries. At his side were Francis of Toledo and

Theophilus Palaeologus, brave warriors who fought furiously. But under the weight of countless Turks they all fell, mown down like corn. The last Emperor of Byzantium lay beneath a heap of corpses. A Turkish soldier recognised him by his boots, cut off his head and ran to exhibit his trophy to the sultan.

16

The Fall of Constantinople

DEFENDING the sea wall, the Greeks continued, as the morning wore on, to harry the enemy with their arrows dipped in boiling pitch. Chamouza's ships were halted by Greek fire, but the Greeks were soon out of ammunition. While the janissaries were despoiling the palace of Blachernai the Turkish sailors succeeded in landing and sacking the Jewish quarter.

Within the city the inhabitants were sleeping peacefully. Suddenly Greek soldiers in flight from the battle ran through the streets, crying:

"The city is taken! The Turks are here!"

The Byzantines refused to believe their ears. How could the God-guarded city fall into the hands of the infidels—and on the very day when they were preparing to celebrate with great pomp the feast of St. Theodosia, virgin and martyr?

But gradually they were forced to awaken to the reality. The Turks were everywhere. The defenders of the Golden Horn had fled; first Cardinal Isidore, disguised as a· beggar, then Grand Duke Notaras and finally the Venetian commanders. Phrantzes himself had given way to panic after the death of his emperor.

The terrified population rushed to the harbour, but the soldiers who had escaped from the Turks had already embarked with all speed aboard the Greek and Italian vessels. There was not enough room for all the fugitives. They crowded on to the quays, they clutched at the ships' sides, they overloaded the vessels until they were on the point of sinking. The captains gave the order to weigh anchor and many of the wretched refugees fell into the water, while others swam until they were exhausted, trying in vain to reach improvised rafts. Although the sultan had promised them his protection, the people of the suburb of Pera did the same, putting out to sea in all their boats. The Turkish ships in the Golden Horn tried to give chase, but a dozen of the Christian ships sacrificed themselves along the chain which they had managed to stretch across the entrance once more. At least the West would learn from the fugitives themselves of the might and ferocity of the Turks.

The crowd was pouring back towards the centre of the town, to St. Sophia. In a few moments thousands of Byzantines—men, women and children; young and old —had found shelter in the huge cathedral. The doors were closed. A priest mounted the steps before the altar. The people prayed fervently.

But soon the heavy bronze doors fell, under the blows of axes and iron bars, and the Turks entered the sanctuary, sword in hand. The screaming crowd rushed hither and thither, vainly seeking an exit, while the janissaries slaughtered every Greek in their path. Then an order was given: enough of bloodshed! The survivors were bound with belts, ropes or leather thongs and led into the Turkish camp: the men first; then the children, snatched from their mothers' arms; and finally the women, groaning at the horror of their fate.

After the captives had left, the janissaries despoiled the church, stacking up the sacred gold and silver vessels, the precious reliquaries and the jewelled crosses. The relics were desecrated, the bones of the saints thrown to the dogs, the consecrated wine poured out on the flagstones. Some of the soldiers amused themselves by putting on the chasubles and lace vestments. They danced round the fires which had been lighted with missals and psalters.

At midday the sultan entered the city by the Gate of St. Romanus, at the head of his guard.

"In two years I will take Rome," he said exultantly.

Passing down the Mesé, he crossed the deserted capitol and the Square of Taurus. He stopped for a moment to drink a little fresh water from the fountain in the Forum of Constantine. As he passed he admired the palaces, porticoes and columns. Yes, it was a beautiful city. Today it was his trophy, tomorrow it would be his capital.

Mohammed II was now passing before the marble and gilded bronze statues representing the emperors of Byzantium who had made the whole world tremble. The sun's rays caressed the mute witnesses of bygone glory.

The Square of the Augusteum was full of joyful janissaries waving their white bonnets and shouting cries of victory. The sultan stopped, impressed by the splendour of the palaces. Then he caught sight of the splendid dome of the church of St. Sophia, of which the Byzantines were so proud that they said it was suspended from Heaven. "That," he thought, "shall be the great mosque of Islam." He imagined it flanked by four minarets and defying the ravages of time.

Reaching the dusty forecourt of the cathedral, Mohammed prostrated himself on the ground. He picked up a handful of dust which he scattered over his turban in token of humility.

"May Allah be praised, He has given us the victory!"

He rose, entered the church and saw the traces of the slaughter. The floor was strewn with corpses; wounded men lay groaning as their blood oozed on to the flagstones. The sultan was sickened. He regretted that he had given his men the right to sack the city.

Near the choir he saw a soldier breaking up a fragment of the marble floor.

"Why are you doing that?" he asked sternly.

The other thought it would be clever to reply: "Is this not an infidel monument?"

"Wretch!"

With a stroke of his scimitar the sultan cut off the man's head. Then he instructed his officers:

"Let all know that I authorised the pillage of private houses, but the public buildings are mine."

Then Mohammed went up to the marble and gold altar, strewn with the fragments of broken crucifixes. He told the Islamic priest, the Imam, to go into the pulpit and read the Muslim prayer:

"In the name of Allah, the gracious and merciful! Heaven and earth sing the glory of the Eternal. . . ."

Then the sultan left the cathedral. He gave orders for the slaughter to cease and for the ruins to be repaired, for the city must come to life again. Despite its fall, Byzantium still made an impression on its conqueror. He decided that from then on the crescent on the Turkish standard would be joined by the star of the three Magi which had twinkled on the imperial banners, in token of divine protection.

When We Recapture the City . . .

ITTLE did its last defenders dream that as the Byzantine empire crumbled a new age was dawning for the West. At mid-day on Tuesday, May 29th, 1453, when Sultan Mohammed II made his entrance into the God-guarded city, the world which had been heir to Greece and Rome came to an end.

During the next few centuries the Turks were to lose, one after another, the European countries they had conquered. The Greeks, free at last, would dry their bitter tears, but Constantinople, the last bastion, would remain in the hands of the Muslims. The walls of St. Sophia bore, not the words of the Gospels, but the verses of the Koran, and five times a day the muezzin called believers to the ritual prayers.

Yet for generations of Greeks, bowed beneath the

Turkish yoke, the liberation of Constantinople was the great hope. Little children heard at their parents' knees beautiful legends foretelling the joyful day when the city would be recaptured from the infidels.

"If you should chance to see, gliding in the clear water of a little stream, seven strange fish, half fried and yet alive, do not be amazed. They are the fish of the poor monk who could not believe that the Turks had entered Constantinople. Squatting by the stream, he was cooking his meal over a wood fire and had already fried the fish on one side. He was about to turn them when he heard the fateful news.

"'Never shall the infidels enter the city!' cried the monk, 'any more than these fish can come back to life!'

"Then with a vigorous flick of their tails the seven fishes leaped out of the boiling oil and into the stream, half fried and half alive. . . . For ever? No! When we recapture the city another monk will come, and the seven fish will allow themselves to be caught by him; and, like the first, he will light his wood fire by the stream and will finish the frying."

*   *   *

Other legends spoke of the last Mass in St. Sophia on that last day of the empire:

"When the Turks entered the cathedral a priest was celebrating Mass. When he saw the infidels coming he had but one idea: to save the consecrated host and the precious blood of Christ from desecration. Taking the holy chalice with him, he mounted the ambo, the pulpit above the choir, and disappeared through a little door which he closed behind him. Unfortunately the Turks had seen him and they rushed after him.

"But when they arrived in the place where the door should have been, they were astonished to see only a bare, smooth surface, without the least sign of an exit! Furious at the deception and determined to get to the bottom of the affair, they battered at the wall and broke their weapons on it in vain.

"'Summon the masons of our army,' ordered the sultan, 'and let them demolish this wall! We shall soon see what there is behind it.'

"The masons arrived with their picks and iron bars and set to work. But despite all their efforts they could not pierce the wall and they had to admit that some secret technique must have been used to construct it.

"'You are incompetent,' shouted the angry sultan, 'and you shall be punished! Let Byzantine masons be summoned.'

"These were hastily brought in and ordered under pain of death to knock down the wall. But they too were unsuccessful!

"For it was God's will, mightier than any human strength, which held the stones together to protect the priest.

"Through the centuries the priest has waited, holding the chalice against his breast, safe from the infidels. But when we recapture the city he will come out through that door, which will open of its own accord. He will mount the altar steps and resume the holy words of the Mass at the very place where they were interrupted."

*   *   *

On that terrible day when so many churches were plundered and so many sacred objects profaned, the Byzantines, so the legend goes, tried to preserve the altar of St. Sophia and the precious relics it contained from the infidels. In this connection a strange story was told:

"On the day when the city was taken people hastened to place the altar on a ship for transport to the country of the Franks, to whom they hoped to entrust it. But on the Sea of Marmara the ship met with a violent storm. As it had been equipped in haste and overloaded, it was unable to resist the waves and sank with its crew and its cargo.

"Thus the altar of St. Sophia escaped sacrilege, not in the way that the Byzantines had hoped, but as God pleased.

"The altar of St. Sophia rests at the bottom of the sea on its bed of sand and shells. But the place where the vessel sank is known to sailors and easily reached. In fact, even when the worst storms whip up the waves round about and make the sea rage, only calm and peace prevail in that place. Sweet odours rise from the smooth and shining surface of the waves, and echoes of angelic songs can be heard. Many skilled divers, collectors of red corals and sponge-fishers have tried to descend to see the wreckage of the vessel. None have reached it. The sea, which is very deep in this place, guards the altar and the relics from all desecration.

"But when we recapture the city, the altar which is engulfed in the sands of the sea-bed will rise to the surface, as a diver rises. It will sail by itself to Byzantium and we shall receive it. We shall take it back to St. Sophia and reconsecrate it, amid hymns of joy, to the Divine Wisdom.

"Then, in the cathedral built by the great Justinian, the gold mosaics will glitter once again, the holy images, the Gospels and the cross will reappear on the marble altar weathered by the waves. . . ."

*   *   *

The last Emperor of Byzantium, Constantine Dragases, was killed, as we know, when the Turks made their attack on the palace of Blachernai. He fell, deserted by his men, but a legend was left to improve upon the cruelty of history:

"When the Turks entered the city our emperor charged on horseback at the head of his guard to halt them. But the infidel hordes were numberless, while the Basileus had only a handful of men about him. Nevertheless, the battle between Christians and Turks was fierce. Sword blows were exchanged, but the fight was too unequal and one after another the emperor's men fell dead or grievously wounded, while Constantine alone, surrounded by the enemy in their thousands, continued to fight on heroically, whirling his sword, slicing and cutting all about him. Suddenly, the infidels gave a cry of triumph: the emperor's brave horse had fallen down dead, throwing its rider to the ground. A great Negro, black as ink, rushed forward brandishing his curved sabre, but his arm was miraculously stayed: an angel of the Lord scattered the Turks with his fiery sword and bore the Emperor Constantine away from his enemies, leaving them dumb with amazement.

"Near the Golden Gate is an underground cave which stretches back below the rocks in a maze of passages and chambers. There the angel hid the emperor, transformed into a block of stone so that none should discover him again.

"There in the shadows the last sovereign of Byzantium awaits the day when the angel of God will come to take him by the hand, bring him back to life and restore him to the world of the living.

"Then the emperor will pick up the good sword with which he fought so bravely long ago; he will leave the cave, and about him the Lord will gather an army of countless thousands. He will enter the city through the Golden Gate, as so many victorious emperors have done before him, and the Turks will flee in terror; they will try to hide in the houses, the palaces and the mosques, but they will not escape their punishment.

"And when we recapture the city, led by our beloved Basileus, we shall not spare a single infidel and there will be such carnage that the Forum of Taurus will be bathed in blood."

Over the centuries these legends, handed down from generation to generation, upheld the hope of liberation of the Christian peoples of the Balkans, who never resigned themselves to the harsh rule of the Turks. The capture of Constantinople roused Europe. How had the Byzantine Empire come to this pass?

History explains the causes of its fall to us, but the legend refuses to admit the harsh reality. An empire which lasted for eleven hundred and twenty-three years, which inherited Greek thought and propagated the Christian faith, could not have fallen thus in a single night into the hands of the infidels. When Mohammed entered the city the sun, it was said, veiled its brightness behind thick clouds in token of mourning.

For us, the date 1453 does not only signify the beginning of the modern era, a new stage in history; it also evokes the memory of a world of grandeur, and all the bitterness of regret.